JORDAN M. ATIN, BARRY FISH & LES KOTZER

The Family WAR

Winning the Inheritance Battle

The Family WAR

Winning the Inheritance Battle

JORDAN M. ATIN
LL.B., T.E.P.

BARRY M. FISH
B.A., B.C.L., LL.B., T.E.P.

LES KOTZER
B.A., (Hons), LL.B., T.E.P.

Continental Atlantic Publications Inc.

3

ISBN 0-9683513-8-7
ISBN 978-0-9683513-8-3

American Inquiries can be made:

c/o Continental Atlantic Publications Inc.
4200 Wisconsin Avenue N.W.
PMB #106-229
Washington, D.C.
20016-2143

All other inquiries can be made:
c/o Continental Atlantic Publications Inc.
7951 Yonge Street
Thornhill, Ontario, Canada
L3T 2C4

Telephone Toll-free (US & Canada) 1-877-439-3999

www.familyfight.com
www.thefamilywar.com

The discussion in this book should not be considered legal or financial advice. Legal and financial advice can only be obtained from a professional in your jurisdiction. Please consult your own professional advisor with respect to any steps you wish to carry out as a result of reading this book. The laws governing the various topics, discussed in this book, will vary depending on the jurisdiction.

Printed and bound in Canada

ABOUT THE AUTHORS

JORDAN M. ATIN is a Certified Specialist in Estates and Trusts Law.

He acts as a mediator and lawyer in estate disputes. He is Senior Associate Counsel to Hull & Hull LLP, one of North America's largest estate litigation firms. A member of The Society of Trust and Estate Practitioners, he has chaired and presented papers at dozens of estate law conferences for the Bar Association, Osgoode Hall Law School and many other professional organizations. Many of his articles are cited in leading Estate Law texts.

BARRY M. FISH graduated from McGill University in the late 1960's with both civil law and common law degrees. He is the senior partner in his law firm, Fish & Associates, which he established in 1973. He is a member of the Society of Trust and Estate Practitioners and has a lengthy experience in the field of estate disputes. Barry, a co-author of The Family Fight, Planning to Avoid it, is a frequent radio and television guest and contributor to various newspapers and magazines. He is married and has two children.

LES KOTZER, a Wills and Estates lawyer since 1989, focuses his practice on avoiding and resolving inheritance disputes. He graduated Law School on the Dean's List. He is a member of the Society of Trust and Estate Practitioners and is co-author of The Family Fight, Planning to Avoid it.

He is also a regular guest on TV and radio across North America.

As well, Les is a professional songwriter. He has co-written the songs on the CD *A Family United- A Family Divided* (Songs to Touch the Heart of the Family). His website is www.familyfight.com. He can be reached at leskotzer@familyfight.com

Acknowledgements

Jordan M. Atin:

I have been fortunate to have so many colleagues assist and support me throughout my professional career. Three deserve special mention. Harold B. Cohen was my first mentor and his early advice continues to influence me. Rodney Hull and Ian Hull provided me with the professional opportunity of a lifetime. I have the privilege of working with them and learning from them everyday. Any success I have had in my professional life is due largely to these three men.

My mother, Dorothy and my late father, Harvey, taught me and my siblings, Mark and Tracey, life's most valuable lesson: how to love and respect one another. I will always be indebted to them.

My wife, Katie is my soul-mate. We are true partners in life's journey.

Les Kotzer:

Sam, Bessie and Sara Handley– You are all in my heart forever. My late mother, Rose and my father, Jack always told me that their greatest gems were not in the bank, but were in the faces of their children. I owe so much to them. My brother, Joel has taught me the meaning of brotherhood. My wife, Miriam is my source of inspiration. Suzie and Michelle- I treasure our time together. My family means everything to me.

Barry Fish:

I am dedicating this book to family, every one of whom has given me the support and inspiration to share what I feel, with as much of the world as I can reach. At the time of first printing, my mom is in her late eighties, a Gold Life Master in Bridge and always seems to smile. Mom, a day doesn't pass when I don't feel that smile of yours. My dear wife Pearl, your endless support drives me on. To my children, Adrian and Joanna, the gift you give me every day that passes, is your endless capacity to care. Finally, to my late Father Abe, who taught me more than words can ever express, the words in this book will never pass before his eyes, but it is in the words of this book that his inspiration will live.

Dedication

For:

Katie, Spencer and Holly, Mark, Tracey, Dorothy,
and in memory of Harvey and Sydney

Miriam, Suzie and Michelle

Pearl, Joanna, Adrian and baby Nadia

"Let him who desires peace prepare for war."
-Flavius Vegetius Renatus

TABLE OF CONTENTS

PREFACE

A Will contains the final words ever spoken by a parent to his or her children.

What does it say to them?

For many children, a parent's Will is interpreted as reflecting something deeper about their lifelong relationship. Those words in black and white are an expression of a parent's confidence or distrust, pride or disappointment in the child. A large gift, or a smaller one, is seen as a reward or a reprimand.

We have all heard of nasty divorces, often between people who have been married for only a few years. A Family War over a parent's estate is like a divorce between siblings. But in the case of an estate dispute, the combatants have grown up together, shared a childhood, and were often close to each other for 30, 40, and in some cases, 80 years.

After a Family War, one client of ours refused to refer to her sibling as her "brother." Instead, she insisted that he be called "my mother's other child."

It is no wonder that disputes over estates develop into some of the most emotionally charged cases that lawyers see.

FOREWORD

Over the next 20 years, it is expected that massive wealth will be passed down from one generation to the next. Tragically, it is a good bet that many brothers and sisters, nieces and nephews, sons and daughters will wage war on one another because death and money form a combustible combination.

Picture your own family tree. Each branch connected to another, sharing a common trunk. After a Family War over an inheritance, one or more of the branches are cut off. They may never grow back.

There could be generations of cousins who will not know each other because their relationship with their extended family was destroyed when their parents or grandparents fought each other over an estate.

Does any person want to leave a legacy of a Family War when he or she dies? Of course not. Yet today, inheritance battles occur with increasing frequency.

Is it possible that siblings who grew up together and looked after each other cannot look one another in the eye after their parents have died?

Could a brother turn his back on his sister, his only living relative, because of how Mom's estate was divided?

Sadly, the answer is yes.

INTRODUCTION

As Wills and estates lawyers, we often see families fighting. Over and over, clients caught in a family inheritance battle tell us that they had assumed this sort of thing could never happen to them.

Our experience proves one thing: It really can happen in *your* family.

WARNING SIGNS: DANGER AHEAD!

What you are about to read are common situations that may indicate that a Family War is looming in your family. If you recognize any of these, beware.

1. Your mother and your sister have a very large joint bank account. In fact, this large bank account represents the money from your father's estate that went to your mother under his Will. The only reason for your sister being named as joint owner is because she lives in the same town as your mother and you live 40 miles away. You have been told that as a joint owner, that joint account will all go to your sister when your Mom dies.

   Will your sister share the joint account with you when Mom dies?

2. Mom always trusted you and you always looked after her. She appointed you under her financial Power of Attorney so that you could help her in managing her financial affairs. Always acting in Mom's best interests, you bought what she needed and made sure she was always provided for in the best way possible. Your sisters, who were spared the burden of managing Mom's affairs, never seemed to mind these arrangements. However, after Mom died, they suddenly began to question many of the expenses that you paid out of her bank account using her Power of Attorney.

You sense a new feeling of mistrust when they insist on a full written accounting from you for the first time.

Are you prepared to answer their questions?

3.   Mom and Dad always managed to settle the rumblings over who would get certain weekends at the family cottage during the summer. Your sister would, if she had her way, take all the holiday weekends for herself, leaving the weekdays for you and your brother. She has never changed her attitude. Although Dad has now passed away, Mom still has the ability to keep her in line. What will happen once Mom passes away? You see trouble brewing.

Will you still be able to use the cottage when you want to?

4.   Your older brother brags about how he is always suing people and winning. For example, he likes to talk about the fact that he sued the store owner for defective merchandise, and of the time that he sued the city because he slipped on some wet pavement. He is proud of the fact that he is always wearing people down until they give in, and he lets you know that he is not afraid to go to court. Your older brother is a bully, and to him, litigation is a game.

Will you be able to stand up to him if he starts a lawsuit over your parent's estate?

5.   Your sister-in-law is very controlling. When your brother got married to her, he stopped coming to family functions. She is also very cold to you. Now you find that your brother is following her lead. Your brother rarely sees Mom anymore.

When Mom dies will she push your brother into a battle with you over Mom's estate?

6.   Mom confides in you, always telling you how much she trusts you. Recently, she has told you that because you are the eldest child, you are the one who will be the best to look after her

estate. She tells you this in confidence, wanting you to promise to say nothing to your brothers and sisters. She then appoints you as sole executor of her estate.

Will your siblings be so jealous that they will look for any way to sue you as Mom's executor?

7.   When you and your siblings get together at Mom's house, everyone always admires the expensive painting in the living room. Mom does not want to make any specific provision in her Will to cover this painting. She believes that all of her children will "work it out."

How will you feel if the painting ends up hanging on your sister's wall?

8.   Your brother lives well above his means. In fact, he has a job that pays nowhere near enough to support his lifestyle. He is swimming in debt, but feels that in the end, he will have nothing to worry about. His reasoning is that his inheritance from your parents will solve all of his financial problems. Your brother is a "waiter" — he is waiting for his inheritance.

Will he fight to get as much as he can to support his lifestyle?

9.   Your sister has moved away and lives on the other side of the continent. Except for a telephone call at Christmas, she has no contact with the family. Mom tells you that it would be unfair for your sister to receive as much as you under her Will. Mom intends to leave your sister a very small amount.

Will your sister accept a lesser amount than you?

10. Everyone always laughs about how bad Dad's memory is. He is always forgetting where he puts his keys. He repeats the same stories over and over again. There are times when he calls you by your brother's name and calls your brother by your name. But now Dad wants to give you the down payment for your new home.

Will your brothers and sisters challenge Dad's gift to you, alleging Dad's lack of mental capacity?

11. You are the only one of your siblings who sees Dad regularly. The others are too busy with their own families. You take Dad to all of his doctor's appointments, you take him shopping, and you take him to do his banking. When it comes time for Dad to make a new Will, he tells you he wants to leave you more than your siblings. He asks you take him to your lawyer.

Will your siblings claim the Will is invalid because you pressured Dad into a making a new Will?

12. Mom and Dad are aging, but doing well at home. They have repeatedly made it clear to you and your sister that if anything happens to them they want to remain at home because they do not like the idea of being in a nursing home. You want to follow Mom and Dad's wishes. Your sister feels that she knows better.

Will a Court have to decide what is best for Mom and Dad?

13. You and your brother disagree about everything. Mom has appointed you and your brother as joint executors of her estate.

What happens after Mom dies and you can't agree?

14. You have always worked hard and earned enough money to live comfortably. Your brother is a no-good slouch who cannot hold a job and lives on welfare. From the way Dad is talking, you get the feeling that he believes that your brother needs the inheritance more than you do.

     Will you be upset and look for ways to get what you think is fair?

15. Over many years, you have built up the family business working side-by-side with Dad while your brother was getting a university education. When your brother occasionally drops in to see you at the business, he tells you how you should "modernize" and make changes in the business. You realize that with all of his university education, your brother knows absolutely nothing about the business. Last month, at a family gathering, Dad told you that he is going to divide everything equally in his Will.

     How are you going to be able to deal with having your brother as your business partner?

16. Mom and Dad gave your sister money for university. They gave you a lot more money to help you buy your new house.

     What happens when your sister finds out that you got a lot more than she did?

17. For years, Mom always talked about what she was going to do in her Will. When you asked her if she ever made her Will, she told you she will get around to it as soon as she has time.

     What if she dies without a Will?

18. Dad believes that if you want it done right then you do it yourself. He fixes his own car and repairs his own house. Now he is going to the internet to find out how to draft his own Will.

What problems will Dad cause by drafting his own Will?

19. After Dad passed away, Mom appointed Uncle Fred as her executor because Uncle Fred was good with finances. Years have now passed and she has decided to name you and your brother as her executors because she no longer has confidence in Uncle Fred. However, she has been procrastinating and you and your brother are still not appointed. Last week, her doctor found her to be mentally incapable. It is now too late for Mom to make a new Will.

Will Uncle Fred follow what you want done with Mom's estate?

20. Mom got remarried three years ago. You are her only child, but her husband has three daughters from his first marriage. You always felt that Mom would protect you if anything happened to her. But now she is going to a lawyer to do her Will and tells you that she is going to leave everything to your step father. You know that this will include your grandmother's heirlooms and very expensive jewellery, which Dad gave to her. She says not to worry because your step father will leave these things to you in his Will.

Will your step father make a Will that respects your Mom's wishes?

21.   Dad appointed you under his financial Power of Attorney and now Dad is incapacitated. You begin to examine all of his assets and liabilities. In his papers you discover Dad's note that your brother borrowed $10,000 from him. You mention this to your brother, who says that he paid that loan off. Your sister swears to you that Dad told her before he became ill that the loan was outstanding. You ask your brother to show proof of payment and he says that he repaid Dad in cash.

Will your sister force you, as your Dad's Power of Attorney, to sue your brother to get the money back?

These warning signs demonstrate how issues that may not be problematic while Mom and Dad are in charge can ultimately turn into a Family War when the parents lose their mental capacity or die. While the parent is alive and healthy, the children's thoughts and feelings are often suppressed and issues are glossed over.   The "referee" parent is still on the scene, keeping a lid on any potential flashpoints. But, when the parent is gone, the restraints are lifted and sometimes these flashpoints explode into a Family War.

WHY WE WROTE THIS BOOK

Our objective is to provide you with enough information so that you have a feel for what it's like to be engulfed in a Family War.

You may have the impression that an estate dispute is like any other lawsuit. But that is not the case. A family estate battle is likely to haunt you for the rest of your life, and your family for generations to come.

Winning a Family War is not like winning a baseball game, where there is a clear winner and loser. Unlike the baseball game where the winner is defined as the one with the most runs, in a family dispute there is far more than money at stake. The party who appears to succeed in winning an estate court case may in the process be depriving himself of something far more valuable—his relationship with his family. One client told us that to him winning "The Family War" meant that, even after resolving the issues in their Mom's estate, he could still talk to his brother, his niece and nephew at a family wedding.

Our book recognizes that some inheritance battles are inevitable. Money, death and family often combine to form a recipe for litigation. Although estate fights are commonly perceived to be just about money, and although in the end money can settle these types of fights, there is almost always more to a "Family War" than just the money.

Many estate disputes are sewn by the seeds of jealousy, greed, thirst for control, bitterness, hatred, and hurt feelings resulting from real or perceived preferential treatment by a parent. Such feelings can erupt over being deprived of personal possessions or a share in the money that was promised by a deceased parent.

Look into the future: Many years have passed since you won "The Family War" against your siblings. Now you are sick in the hospital and your brothers and sisters refuse to visit you.

You won "The Family War," but you lost the family.

WHY YOU NEED THIS BOOK

If you are an executor or a beneficiary, or someone close to the deceased, our book provides tips and strategies for many common estate situations that can ultimately lead to a dispute, including:

a)   You are an executor or Power of Attorney and want to protect yourself from being sued by the beneficiaries. We explain your role and how to fulfill your duties so that litigation can be avoided.

b)   You feel you have been treated unfairly in Mom's Will and do not believe her Will is valid. We discuss the grounds for attacking a Will and other possible ways to get more from the estate.

c)   You are a beneficiary and want to protect your entitlement to Dad's estate from greedy siblings or others wanting a share. *The Family War* outlines your rights and options, provides strategies to assist you and explains what to expect in an estate fight.

d)   You are expecting a Family War to break out over issues like the division of Mom's personal effects. The book provides strategies to prepare for — or head off — the dispute, including ways to reach a settlement and minimize the impact of the fight on your family.

e)   You feel an obligation to stand up and fight for Dad's wishes regarding the family cottage or family business. We canvass options for taking action and strategies for protecting your parent's true intentions.

Regardless of which side you are on, the book recognizes the importance of resolving a Family War as early as possible to minimize its emotional and financial costs for you and your family.

CHAPTER 1

REAL-LIFE FAMILY WAR STORIES

From our experience on call-in television and radio shows, general inquiries, and our public appearances, we hear a lot of Family War stories. The following war stories are based on real-life situations we have encountered. We have altered certain facts or names, where appropriate.

1. *MARY'S CHOICE*

Dad named Mary as the sole executor of his estate.

Mary was one of three children, all of whom Dad loved equally. However Dad knew the personalities of her two brothers well enough to know that his estate would best be looked after by Mary.

To Mary, it seemed that everything was a contest between her two brothers. It had been this way ever since they were all teenagers.

When Dad passed away, he left a Will dividing his estate equally among all three children.

One of the assets Dad left behind was a treasured 1967 Mustang convertible in almost mint condition. Dad and the boys had treated it as their baby. In order to avoid fights Dad kept the keys, so the boys always knew whose turn it was to get that car. Unfortunately, Dad did not specify how that car was to be handled after he died. Now that he had passed away, it was up to Mary to deal with the sensitive issue of which brother was going to get the car.

At first, she thought that common sense would make this an easy matter to resolve. Both brothers were adamant that the car should be theirs, so she tried to work out an informal bidding process. The process quickly turned chaotic when it became apparent that there was no end to it. No matter what one brother offered, the other came back with a higher amount. To Mary, it seemed that one brother would pay almost any price to ensure that the other brother would not get the Mustang.

In order to break the logjam between them, she threatened that if they could not work this out within one week, she would sell the Mustang to someone outside the family. Both believed that she was bluffing. They found out how wrong they were when the car was picked up by a dealer - gone from the family forever.

Naturally, the brothers were angry with Mary, as well as each other. It was just like when they were teenagers and Mary was caught in the middle between them.

Mary told us how much she loved her two brothers and their families. She was in tears when she next related what both brothers had in common: each brother had told her that if she spoke to the other brother, he would never speak to her again.

Mary wondered aloud to us whether that Mustang meant that she couldn't watch her nephew playing football or attend her niece's school graduation, out of fear of losing one of her brothers. She has now realized that her father's Will put her in an impossible position. She told us that she wished that the Mustang, which had given her family so much pleasure, had never been bought by Dad in the first place.

Her parting words were: "Whatever decision I make, I am going to be left with only half a family."

2.   HAIL TO THE CHIEF

Here is what we were told by a caller on a radio talk show a few years ago. We will call her Iris. As in the previous story, we found ourselves listening to a woman who had two brothers. The following is a summary of what she had to say to us and to the listening audience, on that radio show.

After Dad died, Mom's life took a turn for the worse. She moved from their house to a small rented apartment. It was always messy and dirty. Every Saturday, Iris came to Mom's apartment to clean the floors, the kitchen, the bathroom, and to dust. Her twin brothers never had time for any of this and while they gave Mom some money here and there, Mom never seemed to have enough to make ends meet. The twins rarely came to the apartment; it was not an inviting place.

Mom died in poverty, in the middle of the month. Her rent had been covered to the end of the month, but the landlord wanted her stuff out of there as soon as possible. Mom had nothing and left no Will.

Iris asked the boys to help her clean out the place. One of them agreed, and the other had to go out of town. It was agreed among all three that if there was anything of value in the mess they expected to clean up, it was going to be "finders-keepers." No one expected to find anything of value anyway.

Iris and one of the twins came with a pickup truck a few days after the funeral. They had the permission of the landlord to use his garbage bin to throw things out. There was a lot to throw out. The furniture was of little or no value. The fabric on the kitchen chairs was ripped, soiled and worn out. This was typical of almost everything in that apartment.

Iris went through drawers of crumpled clothing, costume jewellery, and the odd public school scrapbook that Mom had kept.

Then—a surprise. While Mom had nothing of value, Dad had kept something secret that none of the kids knew about.

As Iris went through one of Mom's dresser drawers, she found a large envelope. She shook out a bundle of papers wrapped in a few rubber bands.

As she began to look at the papers, her attention was immediately drawn to the White House address of the President of the United

States of America. Franklin D. Roosevelt had personally written a response to a letter written by her late father!

The President was thanking her father for his support during his campaign and for his suggestions! She went on to find other signed letters from several movie stars, sports personalities, congressmen, and state governors.

Iris told us that she never knew that her dad had been such an avid letter writer. She knew that these letters would be very valuable.

She was quick to point out to her brother that they had come to the apartment with the "finders-keepers" agreement. Her brother didn't see it that way. His understanding was: "One for all, all for one." The "finders keepers" was a joke.

After a shouting match between Iris and her one brother, she received a call from the other twin. He took his brother's side.

The next thing Iris knew, she received a registered letter from her brothers' lawyer, which told her that she had, at best, only a one third interest in the papers she had found in Mom's apartment.

Iris told us how hostile her relationship had become with both of her brothers. She found it to be unfair that they suddenly took an interest in Mom's apartment that she had been cleaning for so many years, and that they had gone to the point of putting a lawyer on the case to go after her.

She now had to get her own lawyer. She had tried to settle with her brothers by offering them the letters from the sports personalities and some of the movie stars, but it was the letter from President Roosevelt that the twins wanted.

Because of how greedy her brothers were, she said she would spend anything to make sure they didn't get the letter.

She ended her call saying she was disgusted with her brothers and that she would never speak to them again.

3.   THE ANTLERS

This reported court case demonstrates how emotions can erupt between siblings over the strangest of items. The starting point of the case finds Dad hunting in 1926. Dad encounters a mule deer with a record size set of antlers. He kills it, arranges for the meat to be packed, and keeps the head and the antlers of the animal.

The antlers themselves travelled a relatively simple path over the next 76 years. Dad kept them in the family home and some time in the 1940s mounted them over the fireplace. Dad passed away in 1968. When Dad died, he left seven children, but no Will. The importance of his dying without a Will will quickly become apparent.

In 1973, the antlers were still in Dad's home. His son Don entered the home while his siblings were absent, and removed the antlers. His siblings were aware of this, but at the time there was no court action brought. Years later, however, Don's siblings came across a newspaper article that opened a new chapter in this saga.

The article referred to Don as the sole owner of "World Class" antlers, which had been appraised as being very valuable. Naturally, these were the same ones that were mounted over Dad's fireplace for all those years. Don's siblings were incensed. They demanded the return of the antlers right after reading that article. They were angry enough to retain a lawyer. They now wanted repossession of the antlers and a declaration that they all owned them equally. They brought a lawsuit against Don.

The institution of legal proceedings was not enough to make Don yield one inch from his position. When the judge heard the case, he rendered a decision that all seven children had an equal right to the antlers because Dad had made no Will.

What was so shocking about this case was that Don refused to comply with the order of the judge, even under penalty of being jailed for contempt. Don defied the court order, refusing to give over the antlers. He was jailed for over ten days.

This remarkable case proves that siblings will fight over anything - even deer antlers.

4.   IN DAD'S "OWN" WORDS

After one of our seminars, a lady approached us to tell us this story:

When her Dad died, he left three sons and three daughters. She showed us her Dad's Will, which gave half of the estate to her eldest sister, Marie. The other five split the other half of the estate.

While we had seen many Wills, this one was particularly unusual. Never had we seen anyone express in such detail the justification for his wishes. He referred to each child in succession:

To his eldest son, Dad said that he was proud of him and that he loved him. Dad reminded that son of how helpful he was, but also reminded him of the $30,000.00 he had given him as a down payment on his home. That Will forgave the $30,000.00 and left him 10% of the estate.

To his second son, Dad described how pleasant and charming that son had been to everyone he met ever since he was a little boy. Dad told him how much he loved him, and wished him every success in life. Dad left him 10% of the estate.

To his third son, Dad extended a heartfelt memory of a trip to England the two of them had taken by boat. Dad told him how much he loved him. Dad wished him a good life. Dad left him 10% of the estate.

To his youngest daughter, Dad spoke of how she mellowed in the years that had passed since her rambunctious childhood. Dad told her how proud he was that she grew up to be such a lovely and mature woman. He told her how he loved her and gave her 10% of the estate.

To the middle daughter, the one who approached us, Dad told her how the emotion of seeing her taking her first steps had stayed with him all of his life. He told her that she had earned his trust and for that reason made her a co- executor with her older sister Marie. He told her how he loved her. He left her 10% of the estate.

That left Marie, the daughter who inherited 50% of the estate. Dad told her and all the others why. Dad explained that when his health was in decline, Marie devoted her full time and attention to him and made him her life's priority, as she:

- looked after all of his business and personal affairs;

- sold one property for him and found another home where he could be happy;

- spent months going through files and records and speaking to lawyers and generally helping him in his lawsuit against his separated wife;

- put her career on hold and stayed at home with him and took him to doctor and dentist appointments;

- spent countless hours tracking down pain killers for his backache and dietary supplements and arranging his prescriptions and looked up the very latest in hearing aids for him.

When Dad was recuperating from an accident, he had to spend weeks in an institution for rehabilitation. While all the children came to visit him, Marie was the one who had breakfast and supper with him every single day during his stay. When he came back home, she did all of the housecleaning and laundry and cooking for him. Every week, she took him out for a dinner in order that he would get out of the house. Several times a week Marie took Dad for walks in the shopping mall. She would plan Dad's entire week. She redid the house in order to accommodate Dad. Dad went on and on over more detail, ending up with the comment that he would not have known what to do with the last years of his life, if not for Marie.

Our first impression was that it seemed only fair that Marie get half of Dad's estate considering what she did for him. But then the lady told us something that changed our view entirely. She told us three things: one of which she always knew, and two of which she discovered when her lawyer interviewed the witnesses to Dad's Will:

- Marie exaggerated everything, to the point of sometimes even lying - and everyone in the family knew it;

- Dad's Will was prepared and typed by Marie; and

- Marie brought the witnesses and stood over Dad as he signed the Will.

The lady told us that she and her other siblings would fight to the bitter end to set aside Dad's Will. It turned her stomach that Marie would manipulate Dad's Will to make herself into something she was not. No one had spoken to Marie since the Will was discovered. The lawyers were now involved.

Ironically, our first impression was that this was a rare Will where the Will-maker did all the talking. Unfortunately, now it seemed that it would be the lawyers doing all the talking.

5.   WHOSE HOUSE IS IT ANYWAY?

On a TV show we got a call from Robert.

Robert married a woman who had a son from her first marriage. That son never took to Robert and the two were always at odds with one another. He told us that the son "hated him."

Robert's wife died in a car accident. Her Will left everything to her son, except their home. Robert had the right to live in the home for as long as he wanted to, but when he moved out or died, then the house went to the son.

Robert was responsible to pay the utilities and the taxes and had to maintain the property and do routine repairs. He had to look after the basic wear and tear. The Will made the son responsible to pay for major repairs.

The Will gave the son liberal access to the home. He could visit it every month at a convenient time for Robert. Her wish was that the son be able to check on the house from time to time.

As Robert explained to us, the first year or so after his wife's funeral passed without incident. However the situation began to deteriorate when Robert entered into a new relationship with another woman. Robert's new girlfriend moved into the house with Robert. This infuriated the son to the point where he promised in front of witnesses that he would make Robert's life so miserable that he would be desperate to move out.

The son was true to his word. Every month, the son would appear to go through the home, inspecting its condition. The son would put together a list of repairs that he demanded Robert make. On two occasions, lawyers had to get involved over the use of the BBQ!

It was clear that the son was trying to make Robert's life unbearable, but Robert was equally determined, out of principle, not to give an inch.

A few months later, Robert's girlfriend left him saying she couldn't go on living this way. The battle of wills had had its first casualty.

6.   WILL IN THE WILL

Our last story came from a person we met at a Wills seminar. When we finished our speech, a young man came rushing up to tell us about his personal situation, which involved a vague Will and greed.

The story starts with Uncle Doug, who had two sisters, Fran and Maggie. Fran was very close to Uncle Doug until the day he died. The other sister, Maggie, lived in California, far away from Uncle Doug and Fran.

The story came to us through Fran's son, "William". When Uncle Doug died, William discovered that he was inheriting $75,000.00 under Doug's homemade Will. William had brought the Will with him and showed it to us. The Will read: "To my nephew, William, I give $75,000." The rest of the estate was split equally between Fran and Maggie.

Maggie had a son named "Billy." Billy got a copy of Doug's Will, which referred to the gift to "nephew, William." Although Maggie's son was known as Billy, the fact was that his legal name was "William". Of course, he too was Uncle Doug's nephew. Billy adopted the position that Uncle Doug's Will referred to *him*. Billy decided to claim the $75,000.00.

William told us that he was appalled at Billy's nerve in trying to take advantage of the situation this way. William told us that Billy had never met Uncle Doug. According to William, Maggie and Fran were trying to stay out of the fight between their children.

William told us that he had decided to fight Billy because he couldn't "let him get away with this". He fought for an entire year. He was going to continue even though his lawyer told him that Uncle Doug's gift would end up in the lawyer's pockets if the case proceeded further. He told us that he would rather the money go to the lawyers than any of it going to Billy. He was fighting for what he thought was right.

William hadn't cared about destroying his ties with Billy, since they had never had a relationship to begin with. What William hadn't expected, and what ultimately convinced him to settle, was that his mother, Fran was being drawn into the battle against her sister, Maggie. William didn't want his fight with his cousin to destroy his mother's relationship with her only remaining sibling.

He told us that he had no choice but to settle with Billy.

CHAPTER 2

BEING AN EXECUTOR –

WHAT YOU NEED TO KNOW

1.   DOING IT RIGHT AND AVOIDING TROUBLE

Before discussing Estate Litigation and some of the contentious issues in an estate, it is important to give you an overview of the role and duties of the person looking after the estate - the executor. Often estate litigation occurs because the executor does not fully understand his or her role and responsibilities.

The executor is responsible to the beneficiaries to properly administer the estate. Beneficiaries have the right to review everything that is done and every decision that is made by the executor.

The beneficiaries can sue the executor if he or she has not carried out his or her administration properly. Therefore, for both executors and beneficiaries, it is very important to understand the basic duties of the executor, and how and when the executor can be sued.

2.   FINDING THE WILL

You were told by Dad that his Will names you as executor. Now that Dad has died, where do you find his Will?

Typical places to search for the Will of the deceased would be in his home, in his place of business, in his safe-deposit box or in the custody of the deceased's lawyer or accountant.

Many Wills have been found in unusual places, such as a golf bag, a tool chest, or even under a mattress.   In other cases the Will is simply never found.

In searching for a Will, avoid any preconceptions as to what a Will may look like. For example, depending upon where the deceased lived, a single piece of paper in the handwriting of the deceased and signed by him or her (sometimes called a "holograph Will") might qualify as a valid Will. It is possible that this kind of Will may be overlooked if the person searching for it is expecting to find a formal typed document inside a legal folder. A holograph Will may be strong enough to revoke a previous lawyer-prepared Will.

The person searching for a Will should not throw out documents without obtaining proper advice. What might look like a scrap piece of paper could in fact turn out to be a valid Will.

In your search for the Will, make notes of letters received from lawyers or other information relating to lawyers. Anything helps if it leads you to the lawyer who prepared the deceased's Will. The examination of the bank statements may show the payment of a lawyer's bill, which in turn can help you find the lawyer who drafted the Will. In addition to the lawyer, other good leads may be the deceased's financial planner or accountant.

Once you have found a lawyer who you think may have the Will, there are certain questions you should ask, including:

a) Did that lawyer prepare a Will for the deceased?

b) If he or she did, is the original Will still in his or her office or did the deceased take it away?

c) Did the deceased have any prior Wills that the lawyer prepared for him or her? A prior Will is important if the current Will is challenged.

In the event that the lawyer does not have the Will, there is other information that you can get from that lawyer which may assist you in finding the Will. For example, the lawyer may refer you to another lawyer who may have been retained for the purpose of preparing the Will of the deceased. It is common for a business person to retain one lawyer for corporate and commercial matters and another lawyer to deal with the drafting of the Will.

The lawyer may not have the original Will of the deceased but he may have a photocopy of it. In some jurisdictions, a photocopy of the Will may be recognized as a valid Will under certain circumstances.

You should also keep careful notes of any discussions, including the date you contacted the lawyers or accountants, since the court may ask you to prove that you made reasonable searches to locate the Will.

You should also contact friends and relatives to determine whether the deceased ever discussed making a Will with them.

Sometimes, after exploring all available sources of information, the Will cannot be located. Before abandoning the effort, one last available search option would be to "advertise" for the Will. In many jurisdictions there are publications that are sent to all lawyers in the area. Often, these publications have advertising space where lawyers and law firms request information about missing or lost Wills.

A typical advertisement would read:

> "Anyone having knowledge of a Will for John Michael Doe, of 123 Anywhere Street, please contact SUSAN DOE at (123) 456-7890."

If the lawyer who drafted the Will or who is in possession of relevant information reads the advertisement, he or she will hopefully contact you. Such a contact will refresh the search for the Will or may even lead to its discovery.

Where all efforts to locate the Will lead to a dead end, the estate will have to be dealt with as if that Will did not exist.

3.   FUNERAL AND BURIAL

When someone dies, the most immediate issue is the funeral and burial of the deceased. It should be recognized that the vast majority of Wills are actually silent on the subject of the funeral and burial of the Will-maker.

Where the Will is silent as to the funeral and burial wishes, the family will usually determine the matter of the funeral and burial in consultation with the executor named in the Will. In most jurisdictions, the executor has the final say over funeral and burial arrangements.

The amount of money spent on the funeral must have some reasonable relationship to the deceased's financial circumstances. Therefore, it is very important for the executor to consult the family with respect to the costs of the funeral. If the executor spends too much, the beneficiaries may be upset. If he or she spends too little, the family may be offended.

In most jurisdictions, instructions in a Will relating to funeral and burial are interpreted as guidelines only, as opposed to binding provisions. In these jurisdictions, the executor has authority to reject the funeral directions in the Will. There are numerous legal restrictions on the options for burial. For example, in most jurisdictions, an executor cannot:

- disperse cremated ashes from an airplane over a populated area; or

- bury the deceased in his backyard.

The subject of the funeral and burial can cause disagreements and sometimes lead to court litigation over the obituary, the inscription on a headstone and the disposition of the body or the place of burial.

4.   PROBATING THE WILL

When the funeral and burial issues have been dealt with, the executor must attend to the assets and liabilities of the estate. For the moment we will assume that:

- the person who passed away prepared a Will;

- the Will named an executor; and

- the executor has found the original Will.

In many jurisdictions, the executor's powers come into effect immediately upon the Will-maker's death. However, the executor may have to take legal steps to confirm his appointment.

The topic of probate is complicated and varies greatly from jurisdiction to jurisdiction. The following is a brief overview.

"Probate" loosely defined describes a court process which:

- confirms that the last Will is valid; and

- confirms the authority of the executor named in that Will to carry out his or her duties.

As mentioned previously, the executor's authority to act comes from the Will and not from probate. Therefore, it may be possible for the executor who is named in a Will to deal with the assets of the deceased without having to obtain probate. This will depend on the nature of the assets involved and the requirements of the jurisdiction in which those assets are located.

However, depending on the circumstances, banks that hold custody of the deceased's assets, or purchasers of estate assets, will require the executor to obtain probate from the court.   With court confirmation of the Will, the bank or purchaser is assured that the Will is valid and that the executor has legal authority to deal with estate assets.

In some jurisdictions, if the executor is granted probate he or she will be protected if he or she distributes the estate in accordance with the probated Will, even if that Will is subsequently found to be invalid. Therefore, there may be situations where probate is not strictly required, but it may still be prudent for the executor to obtain probate for that protection.

Because of the complexities of the issues involved, an executor is strongly urged to seek proper legal advice.

As an executor, you are generally only responsible for the deceased's assets that form part of his estate. Where assets pass outside of the estate, the executor is not responsible for their distribution. Common examples of the deceased's assets that pass outside of an estate and do not require probate are:

- jointly held assets with right of survivorship, such as a bank account held in joint names or a house held in joint ownership. These pass directly to the surviving joint owner and not through the deceased's Will;

- assets held in a Living Trust. A Living Trust is a document, separate from a Will, which sets out how assets are to be dealt with during the lifetime and after death of the person creating the trust. Assets held in a Living Trust pass directly to the beneficiaries named in the Living Trust; and

- insurance policies and retirement pension plans that name a beneficiary. These pass directly to the named beneficiary.

5.   FINANCIAL DUTIES OF AN EXECUTOR

a)   Collecting and Securing the Assets

The executor must collect and inventory all of the assets of the deceased. This will typically involve the review of the personal papers of the deceased to determine both assets and the various trails that may lead to assets. For example, bank statements may show automatic deposits or withdrawals, which can signal the existence of one or more investments or a safe deposit box where other assets may be located. The executor may see payments for insurance premiums, which may signal the existence of an insurance policy. Tax returns may indicate dividend income or interest income, constituting further estate assets.

An executor should always obtain an appraisal or valuation of the assets of the estate. In this way, the executor can satisfy the beneficiaries or the court that full value was obtained if those assets are sold. Valuations may also be necessary to satisfy the government taxing authorities of the estate's value.

Most Wills permit an executor to sell estate assets. An executor has a duty to the beneficiaries to maximize the value obtained from the sale of estate assets. A prudent executor will not sell assets to relatives or friends without the consent of the beneficiaries. Any assets that are specifically gifted to a beneficiary in the deceased's Will cannot be sold by the executor.

Depending on what the Will says, the executor may also have the power to postpone the sale of the estate assets until the market value increases, rent them out, or even continue to run the deceased's business.

In most jurisdictions, an executor is not permitted to buy assets from the estate unless the Will specifically allows him to do so. Even then, an executor should obtain the beneficiaries' consent or get court approval before buying assets from the estate.

The executor would be wise to investigate whether any of the deceased's assets were held in the name of someone else. For example, the deceased may have put legal title to property in the name of a relative or friend with either a formal or informal agreement that the property really belongs to the deceased. This arrangement is often referred to as a "trust arrangement." This is sometimes attempted for tax planning or creditor proofing purposes. Under these arrangements and other similar arrangements, the true owner of the property is not evident on the surface. Therefore, a wise and prudent executor should investigate the affairs of the deceased to determine if any property was held by another person in trust for the deceased.

The executor should determine whether the deceased had loaned money or specific assets to others. The executor should search and make inquiries to determine if there are any promissory notes, mortgages or other evidence of debt. The executor is responsible for making demands for payment or, where reasonable, starting collection proceedings on behalf of the estate.

The description of these functions is not exhaustive, but serves to illustrate what the executor must do as part of his functions in collecting and securing the assets of the estate. The executor should make an inventory of all the deceased's assets, including personal items. This is necessary in order to get a reasonable estimate of the value of the estate. In arriving at such an estimate, a prudent executor will usually retain the services of a professional appraiser.

To avoid losses and a potential lawsuit against him or her, the executor should secure assets by arranging for appropriate fire and theft insurance, and liability insurance. He or she may also change locks and place valuable or perishable items in storage. In certain cases, it is recommended that the executor hire security guards to protect very valuable items.

If the executor does not properly protect estate assets, he or she may be liable to the beneficiaries if these assets are destroyed, damaged, missing or stolen. Similarly, an executor is at risk of being sued if he or she fails to discover an asset of the deceased that should have been discovered.

Executors are often confronted by family members requesting an asset located in the deceased's home. A beneficiary may phrase the request as:

- wanting a memento of the deceased;

- seeking to retrieve an asset that he or she claims was loaned to the deceased; or

- retrieving an asset allegedly promised or gifted to him or her by the deceased.

These requests should be dealt with cautiously by an executor. They may seem reasonable at the time. However, weeks or months later the executor may be confronted by conflicting claims of other beneficiaries to those very assets. Accordingly, before an executor gives away these assets he or she should get legal advice and perhaps the consent of the other beneficiaries.

b)   Paying the Debts

The executor is responsible for paying the deceased's debts. This must be done before distributing the balance to the beneficiaries.

Some debts are easy to determine, such as credit card balances and bank loans.

However, not all debts fall into this category. Sometimes the estate is faced with a claim that may be exaggerated or a claim that may not be legitimate at all.

The cautious executor must take steps to find all of the deceased's legitimate debts. Usually, he or she will place an advertisement in a local newspaper requesting that any creditors of the estate contact him or her within a period of time, such as thirty days. Some jurisdictions will require that the advertisement for creditors be placed on more than one occasion, such as once a week for three weeks. The executor should keep proof of the advertisement to protect him or herself and the estate.

The claimant must satisfy the executor that the claim is legitimate. When deciding whether to fight a creditor's claim, the executor will have to consider the legal costs of opposing the claim. If the executor rejects the claim and the creditor ends up taking the estate to court, the legal costs of defending the claim in court could end up depleting more estate assets than the claim itself. This would expose the executor to arguments from the beneficiaries that he or she acted unreasonably in not settling the claim out of court. Therefore, the executor might wish to take some direction from the beneficiaries in deciding whether to expend estate funds on a legal defence or settle the claim out of court. Due to the difficulties in proving or disproving claims, an executor should be cautious before paying any alleged creditor or taking aggressive steps to defend the claim. Otherwise, the executor risks personal liability.

c)   Following the Will

The executor must carry out the Will-maker's intentions as expressed in the Will. To illustrate this, imagine that you are named as executor in your father's Will. The Will requires you to distribute his assets as outright gifts equally to each of your siblings. You cannot change your father's Will, even if you don't agree with it.   For example, if you are upset with your brother, if you dislike the man your sister married, if you feel a gift in the Will is unreasonably and unfairly generous, if you know your brother is a gambler or drug addict, you have no choice but to give the gifts set out in Dad's Will. Similarly, if your Mom's Will left a gift to a charity that you do not approve of, you have no choice but to follow the instructions in her Will.

d)   Investing Estate Funds

When the executor sells the estate assets or liquidates the deceased's bank accounts, he or she deposits those proceeds into a bank account in the name of the Estate. This is commonly referred to as "the estate account". Bank accounts do not generally pay very much interest. Since the executor's job is to maximize the estate for the beneficiaries, the executor should not, generally, keep large amounts sitting in the estate account. Even if the money is going to be disbursed shortly, it may make sense to invest most of the estate funds in short-term, very safe, but higher yielding investments. Money Market mutual funds, Investment Certificates or CDs may be appropriate in these situations.

Sometimes, the Will requires that money be held in trust by the executor for many years.   During the time the executor is holding the money, he or she should be investing it.   Depending on the situation, the executor may have to balance the need to grow the capital of the money while at the same time providing for interest.

In many cases, the Will does not provide any guidelines for the executor when making investment decisions. In most jurisdictions, the law requires that an executor must invest "prudently", but does not specifically list what investments are prudent. Therefore, it is usually recommended that the executor obtain professional investment advice when deciding how to invest estate funds.   In these jurisdictions, if the executor invests the estate funds prudently, he or she is not generally liable for any loss to those investments.

Beneficiaries will want to know how the executor is investing the estate money.   If the money is just sitting in the estate bank account earning very little interest, the beneficiaries may be in a position to seek a reduction in the executor's compensation or even seek damages from the executor. Similarly, if the investments made by the executor are not prudent, such as putting all the estate money into very risky investments, the executor may be on the hook if the investments lose significant value.

e) Making Decisions

In some cases, such as where the beneficiaries are young children, disabled adults or spendthrifts, the Will-maker may not want them to get their inheritance right away. In these situations, a lawyer will often advise that a trust be set up in the Will to protect the money for these beneficiaries. The money is held and invested by the executor.

However, the Will-maker does not have a crystal ball. It is not always possible for the Will-maker to know exactly what the beneficiary's needs will be in the future. Therefore, a Will-maker may want to give his or her executor the power to decide when a beneficiary should get money from the trust. For example, a parent providing for young children may want the executor to have the power to decide how much the child gets for schooling, medical care or day-to-day living expenses. In such cases, the executor will have the ability to make decisions regarding when the beneficiary is entitled to money and how much the beneficiary will get from the trust. The power to make decisions is often referred to as "discretion".

Some Wills give the executor discretion to pay income generated by the trust investments, and other Wills permit the executor to distribute both principal (often referred to as "capital") and income from the trust to the beneficiary.

This power to decide how much of the income or capital to pay to a beneficiary is often called an "encroachment" power.

Some Wills create trusts for a limited period of time, such as withholding the outright gift of capital to a beneficiary until he or she reaches age 25. Other Wills establish trusts that go on for the lifetime of the beneficiary, such as in the case of a severely disabled beneficiary.

However, even if the executor is given "absolute" or "unfettered" discretion over the trust, the executor cannot make any of these decisions in bad faith or for the wrong reasons. In one case, an executor refused to give the beneficiary money because he did not approve of the beneficiary's marriage to someone of a different religion. The court found that the executor acted in bad faith and for the wrong reasons. The court forced the executor to give the beneficiary money from the trust. Therefore, it is crucial for the executor to understand what rights and powers he or she has under the Will before making any decisions.

Whenever money is held in a trust, there are two separate classes of beneficiaries, each with different and competing interests. One is the beneficiary entitled to the money while he or she is alive, or until a certain date or age as set out in the Will. We will refer to this class of beneficiary as the "Primary Beneficiary." The other is the beneficiary who will inherit the money when the Primary Beneficiary dies. We will refer to this class as the "Secondary Beneficiary". The legal term for the Secondary Beneficiary is the "Remainderman."

- Investments made by the executor with estate assets; and

- Anticipated liabilities of the estate.

The executor should keep records of all payments made by the estate, by way of invoices, bank and credit card statements or other proof of expenditures. Additionally, the executor should keep copies of any appraisals or valuations of estate assets to prove that he or she obtained proper value for them. He or she should also keep copies of all estate investment documents.

6. DISTRIBUTING THE ESTATE

We are at the point where the debts and taxes of the estate have been paid by the executor. He or she now has to distribute the remaining assets of the estate in accordance with the terms of the Will.

Estate assets do not belong to the executor in his or her own right. He or she holds the estate assets for the benefit of the beneficiaries.

It should be recognized that an executor can also be a beneficiary. This often happens when a spouse appoints his or her spouse as the executor and sole beneficiary of the estate. In this case, the executor in fact has the right to all of the assets once the debts and the taxes of the estate have been paid.

Some gifts in a Will are in the form of assets, such as a clock, car or a piece of real estate. Other gifts are stated in terms of an amount of money. These types of gifts are often referred to as "bequests" or "legacies." The executor distributes these gifts first.

After the debts and taxes have been paid and these legacies are dealt with, whatever part of the estate that is left over is called the "residue" of the estate. Professionally drafted Wills always give the residue of the estate to a single beneficiary or multiple beneficiaries. The residue is given away to the beneficiaries using "shares" or percentages. These beneficiaries can be individuals or charities. Usually, the professionally drafted Will recognizes the possibility that a named beneficiary might die before the Will-maker dies, and alternate beneficiaries are named in one form or another.

a)   Timing of Distribution

The most common question an executor hears from the beneficiaries is "When do I get my inheritance?"

The timeframes for distributing the estate will vary from one jurisdiction to another. For example, there are some jurisdictions that provide for an "executor's year," meaning a period of 12 months from the date of death. The executor must conduct his or her administration reasonably and prudently as dictated by the circumstances.

The executor will almost always be faced with the conflict between obtaining confirmation from the government and creditors that all of the taxes and debts have been paid on the one hand, and the demands of the beneficiaries to distribute the assets on the other. It is very common for an executor to resolve this problem by making a partial distribution to the beneficiaries, ensuring that enough is held back in the control of the executor to fund the tax and debt obligations that may arise. In due course, after all the taxes and debts have been paid and the estate is fully clear, the executor will then make a final distribution to the beneficiaries.

It is common for all of the beneficiaries who receive interim and final payments from the estate to sign a release that acknowledges the payments. These releases protect the executor from any future claims by the beneficiaries. Beneficiaries should be encouraged to obtain legal advice before signing any release. This way, the beneficiaries cannot later claim that they did not understand the legal effect of the release.

b)   Assets not owned by the Deceased

Beneficiaries sometimes demand delivery of assets that the executor has no power to distribute.

An executor cannot distribute something that the estate does not own.

Where, for example, the home of the deceased contains furniture or works of art that were either loaned to the deceased, or perhaps belonged to the deceased's child or step child, the executor has no authority to deal with these assets. These assets will not be part of the estate.

This type of issue can easily arise in a situation where there are children from the deceased's first marriage fighting against the deceased's second spouse. Each side may argue that they and not the deceased were the owner of certain personal items. Of course, the executor must rely on proper and sufficient evidence of ownership before acting. Otherwise, he or she can be personally liable if he or she gives the assets to the wrong person.

c)   Circumstances that Alter Distributions

Circumstances which occur after the Will is made can change the distribution of assets.

Let's look at a simple example: John's Will contains a gift of John's Porsche to Bob.

Depending on the wording of the Will and where you live, if Bob dies before John, the Porsche does not go to Bob's estate or his heirs. Instead, the gift of the Porsche "fails" and the Porsche may be distributed as part of the rest of John's estate.

What if Bob survived John, but John sold the Porsche and acquired a motorcycle before he died? Bob gets nothing under this clause of John's Will because it referred specifically to his Porsche. This means that Bob does not get John's motorcycle or the cash equivalent of the Porsche.

The identical principle applies to real estate such as a home or cottage.

7.   EXECUTOR'S COMPENSATION

The beneficiaries will want to know whether the executor is going to be compensated for his or her work. The executor is generally entitled to be paid for administering the estate. In some jurisdictions, the executor is entitled to a percentage of the estate. For example, in one jurisdiction, an executor is entitled to 5% of the estate.

In other jurisdictions, the executor is entitled to "reasonable" compensation. The amount of time spent by the executor, the size and complexity of the estate, and other practical issues are often accepted as factors to determine what a reasonable fee will be. Where the beneficiaries dispute the executor's claim for compensation, a court will set the fee.

The court may take into account any mistakes made by the executor when determining compensation. For example, if the executor incurred penalties for the estate because he or she filed the tax returns too late, the court might reduce the compensation by the amount of the penalty.

Where a family member is the executor, the matter of compensation can be a delicate issue. In some cases, the work is simply done out of love or moral obligation and the executor may wish to waive all of the compensation. While an executor may intend to waive compensation, it is best not to advise the beneficiaries of that intention at the outset of the administration. As we have seen, being an executor can be a very difficult, time-consuming and financially risky job. A beneficiary who is told at the outset that the executor will not be charging compensation will likely hold that executor to his or her word. Should the executor encounter unforeseen time commitments, problems or personal liability in the administration that causes him or her to change his or her mind, he or she will find it difficult to convince the beneficiaries that compensation is warranted. Therefore, an executor is wise to keep the compensation issue open until the conclusion of the administration.

8.   The Risk of Being an Executor

As we have seen, being an executor is not an easy job. It requires a great deal of time, effort and responsibility and may involve potential personal risk.   Here are some examples of potential minefields that an executor may face:

- Unpaid income taxes

In most jurisdictions, if the executor makes a distribution to the beneficiaries without leaving enough in the estate to pay all estate taxes, he or she may be on the hook to pay those taxes out of his or her own pocket.

- Creditors' claims

Imagine paying out interim bequests to beneficiaries under pressure from them, only to find out that the interim payments did not leave enough money to pay the estate's debts. The estate's creditors could turn to the executor to collect the debts from him or her.

- Loss or damage to estate property

What if the deceased owned stocks or shares when the executor took over? If those stocks lose value before the executor sells them, the beneficiaries may be able to sue the executor for the loss to the estate. What if the jewellery and antiques, which the executor keeps under lock and key, go missing? He or she is left to shoulder the blame amid allegations of being careless, negligent or, even worse, accusations that he or she took the missing assets.

- Being caught in the middle between squabbling beneficiaries

Imagine having to make a decision among your bickering siblings, knowing that if you sell the cottage you will upset your sister and if you keep the cottage you will upset your brother.

Keeping this in mind, if you have been named as an executor, and do not wish to take on the job, can you resign?

9.   RESIGNATION OF EXECUTOR

Depending on the circumstances, you may not be able to resign as the executor.

Certainly, at the outset, before taking any steps to administer the estate, most jurisdictions allow you to decline your appointment. You should see a lawyer to help you formalize the resignation and advise you on providing the appropriate notice of your resignation to the beneficiaries.

There are consequences following your resignation. The alternate executor named in the Will becomes the one to carry out the obligations of administering the estate.

If there was no alternate executor named in the Will, then the beneficiaries have to agree on an administrator to be appointed by a court. If there is no agreement among the beneficiaries, the estate will be brought to the point of court litigation, and the fight will be over who will be appointed by the court.

In some jurisdictions, there are circumstances that may prevent you from resigning as executor without getting a court involved. For example, depending on where you live, an executor who contacts creditors on behalf of the estate or who collects estate assets will not be able to resign without a Court Order. In this example, until the executor is formally removed by a court, he or she may not be able to avoid personal liability.

If after reading this you are still willing to take on the job of executor, you are cautioned to take great care in your tasks. You are well advised to retain the services of an estates lawyer to help you.

Up to this point, we have discussed the role and duties of an executor in an estate. We will now turn our attention to what happens when things go wrong.

CHAPTER 3

WHAT IS ESTATE LITIGATION?

1. INTRODUCTION

Estate litigation, more often than other types of litigation, is a process that can embroil entire families. Even family fights over small matters have the potential to result in a Family War.

It will be helpful at this point to summarize the usual types of disputes that can result in estate litigation, and later in this book we will look at these matters in more detail.

a)   One of the most common types of Estate Litigation is the Will Challenge or Will Contest. In some areas, this is also referred to as "Probate Litigation." A family member, friend, or even a charity, believes that the last Will of the deceased is not valid. If the Will is proven to be invalid, a prior Will then becomes the official last Will.

b)   If the Will is valid, certain people may still have a claim against the estate even if they were not named as beneficiaries. Spouses, dependant relatives and caregivers can all make legitimate claims against the estate.

c)   Another type of estate litigation calls into question the executor's handling of the estate. Sometimes executors mismanage the estate assets or do not act properly. If this results in the beneficiaries receiving less than they should, the beneficiaries are entitled to have a judge review the actions of the executor and even replace the executor.

d)   Sometimes the wording of the Will is not easily understood. If the beneficiaries' lawyers are not sure what the wording means, a court will have to interpret it for them.

e)   An increasing trend is "Capacity Litigation," which deals with issues relating to mentally incapable people. This often involves disagreements over the health care of the incapable person, Powers of Attorney, the selection of a guardian or conservator to manage the incapable person's finances or an audit of the guardian's actions.

2.   PARTIES INVOLVED IN AN ESTATE BATTLE

The words "court fight," or litigation, are likely to elicit the image of two parties, each of whom retain lawyers to battle out whatever the issue is between them. This perception may be reasonable in the context of other litigation, such as a contract dispute.

However, when an estate becomes the subject of a dispute, the effect of such a dispute is often likely to involve all members of an entire family. What is especially unfortunate is that the family members who ultimately become embroiled in such a fight could have been very close to one another at an earlier point in time. Images of siblings walking to school together, family birthday parties and picnics are most likely to be shattered with the receipt by one sibling of a letter from his or her sibling's lawyer.

When a family becomes involved in estate litigation, separate lawyers may be needed for certain family members. At this point it would be helpful to examine how the various needs for legal representation arise in the context of adults, minors, the unborn, incapable persons and charities.

a)   Adults

Take a simple example involving three adult siblings. Dad made a Will in 1999 naming his three children, John, Bob and Sue, as equal beneficiaries. Dad changed his Will in 2004, cutting Sue out because they had a falling out. Sue decides to challenge the 2004 Will.

John, Bob and Sue are all parties to this litigation: Sue is the challenger of the Will and John and Bob are defending the 2004 Will.

b)   Minors

Those who are under the age of majority, referred to as "minors," do not have the legal capacity to represent their own interests in an estate fight.

In some jurisdictions, the government appoints a lawyer for the purposes of representing the interests of the minor child.   These lawyers will not always agree with the decisions of that minor's own parents. The lawyers will act independently in what they feel are the best interests of the minor, even over the objections of his or her parents.

To use the example above, let us assume that John died before his dad, leaving two young children. Those minor children would have the right to defend the 2004 Will in the place of their father as parties to the litigation. As minors, they cannot represent their own interests and an adult relative or a government lawyer must be appointed to represent them in settlement negotiations or litigation.

In some jurisdictions, disputes involving minors cannot be settled without a court approving any proposed settlement.

c)   The "Unborn"

Believe it or not, in estate litigation children who have not even been born yet sometimes need their own lawyers.

For example:
Sam is married to Judy. They have two adult children, Ben and Michael. Neither Ben nor Michael has any children of their own.

Sam's estate is held in trust for Judy's lifetime. His Will says that when Judy dies, whatever is left in the estate goes to Ben and Michael, *if* they are alive when Judy dies. If either Ben or Michael dies before Judy, their children (who have not yet been born when Sam dies) would be beneficiaries under Sam's Will.

Those unborn beneficiaries may have to be represented by the government or some other representative. The representative of the unborn beneficiaries may need to hire a lawyer separate from Ben and Michael.

d)   Incapable Persons

Some estates involve beneficiaries who are mentally incapable. Because they are incapable, they are not able to represent themselves in estate litigation. It is usual for the court to appoint someone to act on their behalf. In some jurisdictions, the government may represent an incapable person in estate litigation.

The following example illustrates how easily this type of situation can arise. Husband and wife each make a Will leaving their estates to one another. Several years later, the wife develops Alzheimer's disease, which causes her cognitive abilities to deteriorate to the point where she is mentally incapable. The husband then makes a new Will cutting out his wife and leaving his estate to another person. The wife may have rights in some jurisdictions to claim against her husband's estate. Someone must be appointed to protect her legal rights.

It is entirely possible that a family of five involved in a Family War could be represented by four or even five separate lawyers.

e)   Charities

Charities are frequently named as beneficiaries in Wills, and in many cases, they are parties to estate litigation.

They, like other beneficiaries, have rights, and will defend these rights, even if it means going to court. They have the right to be informed by the executor as to the administration of the estate.

They will also defend their interests in the estate if the Will is subject to attack. For example, a father leaves his estate to a charity rather than to his child. If that child launches an attack against that Will, the charity will, in all likelihood, forcefully defend that Will.

If a charity is left a share of an estate, it will want to ensure that the executor is properly administering the estate and maximizing the charity's interest.

For all of these purposes, charities will retain their own lawyers.

A charity can also become involved in estate litigation where it is not properly identified in the Will. For example, there was one case where a gift was left to an entity identified as "a dog foundation." That name did not identify any registered charity. As a result, more than one charity claimed the gift. It was settled out of court, with the estate being split among several animal-related charities.

In many jurisdictions, the government has a department that protects the rights of charities. Therefore, in those jurisdictions a government lawyer may become involved in estate litigation involving charities.

3. *TYPES OF ESTATE DISPUTES*

a) Contesting the Will

A Will may be contested when a person or charity with a financial interest in the Estate believes that the Will is not valid. A challenge to the validity of a Will may be based on one or more of the following legal grounds:

- That the Will-maker did not have the mental capacity necessary to make the Will;

- That some person was unduly influencing or coercing the Will-maker to make the Will;

- That the Will was not properly signed or witnessed;

- That the signature on the Will was forged; or

- That the Will was revoked, and is, therefore, no longer valid.

Whenever a party contemplates contesting a Will, he or she must consider what will happen if his or her challenge is successful and a court rules that the Will is invalid. Where a Will is found to be invalid, the previous valid Will of the deceased will govern the Estate. Before challenging a Will, the challenger must be sure that he or she does better under the previous Will than under the Will he or she is considering challenging. Otherwise, his or her challenge will backfire. If there is no previous Will, the challenger must then consider where he or she will stand under inheritance laws, which distribute the assets of a deceased person who dies without a Will. Such laws are usually governed by the jurisdiction in which the deceased permanently resided at the time of his death. Inheritance distribution laws vary from jurisdiction to jurisdiction.

Wills are amended from time to time for various reasons, such as revoking one or more particular gifts, or replacing, removing or adding one or more executors. A change to a Will is usually known as a "codicil."

While a particular party may acknowledge that the original Will is valid, he or she may find reason to challenge the codicil.

For example, a person made his original Will at the age of 50 and made a codicil 35 years later at age 85. In this case, the passage of time may have affected his health, mental capacity, or his family relationships. There may be an acknowledgement of the validity of the original Will, but a challenge to his codicil.

The reasons and grounds for contesting a codicil are similar to the reasons and grounds for contesting a Will.

b)   **Claims Against the Estate**

Even where a Will is valid, there are nevertheless other types of estate litigation that can arise. Claims can be brought by parties who were either left an amount in the Will that they feel was inadequate, or who were not named in the Will at all. The treatment of such claims will vary depending upon the jurisdiction that governs the estate. Generally speaking, examples of this type of claim may be summarized as follows:

(i)   Claims by the deceased's dependants to relief or financial support from the estate. The legislation will vary from jurisdiction to jurisdiction, but the law will generally focus on those relatives who had been supported or who were entitled to be supported by the deceased at the time of his or her death. Such "dependants" may be entitled to receive money from the estate under certain circumstances.

(ii) Claims by spouses who are disappointed by their treatment under their spouse's Will. In some jurisdictions, there are community of property laws that provide that the spouses are, in essence, partners in the marital property. Depending on where you live, each spouse may be entitled to his or her half of the family property regardless of the provisions of the Will. The spouse may sidestep the Will, electing instead for entitlement under the law.

(iii) Often there are persons who have provided care to the deceased while he or she was alive. Sometimes, there is an understanding between the deceased and the caregiver that compensation to the caregiver will be paid when the deceased dies. Often, these understandings are not reflected in the deceased's Will. The law may recognize the time and attention devoted by the caregiver if appropriate evidence is furnished to the court hearing the matter. Claims that are properly proven in this manner will be ordered to be paid out of the estate even where the Will is silent or inadequate in this regard.

c)   Claims Involving the Executor

Another form of estate litigation involves claims by beneficiaries or creditors of the estate against the executor. One example is where the executor has not given the beneficiaries a proper accounting of the estate. In this situation, the beneficiaries may be able to get a Court Order forcing the executor to properly account to them. In other cases, beneficiaries or unpaid creditors may ask the court to order that the executor reimburse the estate for not properly preserving estate assets. Other examples of claims against executors are mismanagement of the estate and failure or delay in properly distributing estate assets. In the most severe circumstances, beneficiaries may ask the court to remove the executor entirely and appoint a new one.

d)   Court Interpretation of a Will

Yet another type of estate litigation involves situations where a Will contains language that is unclear. When it comes to the question of expressing intentions in a Will, two comments come to mind.

The first comment is that Wills are documents written for lawyers and judges, not for lay persons. The wording in the Will may have been clear to the Will-maker himself; however, if the lawyers who are representing the executor or beneficiaries are unsure about the meaning of the words, they may be forced to go to court to have the Will interpreted.

A non-lawyer may think that the legal language used in a Will is wordy or confusing. However, the wording used must be very precise to avoid involving the court in having to interpret the Will. Accordingly, to address these requirements, lawyers use language that has developed very precise meaning. The meaning of these terms has been tested and confirmed over decades or even hundreds of years through court interpretation.

The second comment is that if two parties can read the same provision and come to two different conclusions, there is likely to be a problem. To solve the problem there must either be an agreement between the parties as to the Will's meaning or a Court Order to clarify what the words in the Will mean.

e)   Disputes Involving Mentally Incapable Persons.

Not all estate litigation results from the death of a person. Many people do not realize that mental incapacity can lead to estate litigation during the incapable person's lifetime.

In many jurisdictions, the law permits a mentally capable person to make a document designating another person to carry out certain functions on his behalf.   That document is commonly called a "Power of Attorney."   If the person becomes mentally incapable, a valid Power of Attorney directs who can make financial or personal care decisions on behalf of the incapable person.   That person is called an "Attorney."   It must be borne in mind that in this context "Attorney" does not mean lawyer. It means the person appointed as a representative under a Power of Attorney.

Estate litigation involving incapable people can be divided into two main categories:

A.   Where No Power of Attorney Exists

Where a person loses his mental capacity without having previously prepared a proper Power of Attorney, problems can arise. Without a proper Power of Attorney in place, there is no one designated to automatically stand in the shoes of the incapable person to carry out financial decisions on his or her behalf.

With no Power of Attorney in place, a dispute can arise when more than one person applies to court or the government to become the incapable person's representative. This position is often termed a "guardian" or "conservator." Disputes can arise over how much money should be spent to support the lifestyle and comfort of the incapable person.

There can even be a dispute as to whether the person alleged to be mentally incapable is, in fact, legally incompetent.

In terms of medical treatment and personal care, the views of family members may differ in terms of path of treatment, life support, resuscitation, pain management, and other medical decisions.

B.   Where a Power of Attorney Exists

Even with a Power of Attorney in place, estate litigation is still possible. Family members may challenge its validity in a manner similar to a challenge to a Will.

Where the Power of Attorney is acknowledged as valid, litigation can still result. Like an executor, a person acting under a Power of Attorney (the "Attorney") is regarded in law as a trustee. The Attorney must act in the best interests of the incapable person. Where the Attorney is looked upon as failing to fulfil this obligation, he or she is at risk of his or her authority being challenged and incurring personal liability. His or her liability is similar to that of an executor.

CHAPTER 4

ESTATE LITIGATION – IN DEPTH

Now that the subject of the various types of estate dispute has been introduced, a more detailed examination is in order.

1.   CONTESTING THE WILL

Due to depictions in movies and on television, a challenge to the validity of a Will is the most recognizable type of estate litigation. As previously mentioned, a Will can be challenged on a number of different legal grounds.   Let's now examine those grounds of attack:

a)   Mental Incapacity of the Will-maker

Age and disease often diminish mental capacity.   Incapacity is a matter of fact, and the proof of that fact can be complex and unpredictable.

An 80-year-old father changes his Will, reducing the amount given to his son and increasing gifts to various charities.   When he learns about Dad's new Will after Dad dies, the disgruntled son feels that his father was unfair and unreasonable.   The son believes his father's new Will is totally out of character and is considering challenging the Will.   The son should be aware that the law is not liberal when it comes to overturning a Will.   To the disgruntled son, his father's unexplained shift in thinking and attitude, and the resulting changes in his Will may be surprising, unwelcome and out of character. Nevertheless, none of this constitutes proof of his father's incapacity. To prove incapacity, the evidence should show whether the person who made the Will:

- understood the nature of a Will;

- knew the nature and extent of his or her assets; and

- was aware of the people who one might reasonably expect to be beneficiaries of his or her estate.

Some cases are clear cut and there are no issues relating to the capacity of the Will-maker. More often than not, however, there are at least two sides to the story. Here is a typical example.

A daughter who was very close to her father expected him to split his estate equally among her and her brother and sister, even though the two other siblings had been distant from Dad. The daughter is close enough to her Dad to know his medical situation. She takes Dad on an afternoon drive to the beach that Dad has loved all his life. She feels saddened as she sees, and not for the first time, just how disoriented he is. She hears Dad ask her if they are near a certain store that he likes, and she knows that the store he is speaking of is in another city. She hears Dad speak of stopping by his office on the way back, knowing that a quarter of a century has passed since he retired.

Months after that occasion, Dad makes a new Will, using a lawyer whose name is not familiar to her. Dad passes away within the year. The daughter receives a registered letter indicating that she has been given $20,000 in her Dad's last Will. She knows that Dad made that Will well after that sad drive to the beach. She knows that his estate is worth well over half a million dollars. She is so upset that she wants to bring legal proceedings to declare that Will null and void. She seeks advice as to what her legal situation will be if her challenge is successful.

Meanwhile, her brother has been seeking his own legal advice. The full picture of the case is not known until the notes from the lawyer who drafted Dad's Will are disclosed. It turns out that Dad also kept a record of his thoughts and intentions, which comes out in the lawsuit. On the brother's side, what emerges is that he cared for his Dad as much as the daughter that we just read about. The records show that Dad had left her $20,000 because he had given her a home during his life, and that the home was worth over $400,000. The brother also produces medical evidence that shows that Dad did have sufficient mental capacity to make a Will, despite the odd day where Dad became disoriented and had some minor memory lapses.

The litigation proceeds like a chess game.

The daughter counters with evidence to support her argument that Dad had insufficient capacity to make that Will. The brother, defending the validity of the Will, produces further evidence to prove his case. For example, the brother produces an affidavit from Dad's former secretary to show that, even though Dad retired 25 years ago, he would still periodically stop by his former office to say "Hi."

Both sides are driven to produce evidence to support their positions.

Witnesses are interviewed by the parties. The daughter has as a witness, someone who lives on Dad's street, who says Dad rarely came out of his house and never said hello. On the other hand, the brother has evidence from another person who lives near Dad who was aware of everything that the daughter's witness said. However, he explains that the reason for Dad not saying hello was because that person always addressed Dad by the wrong name, and that Dad wondered why he could not get his name right. The brother's witness tells of how he and Dad watched political shows on TV together and discussed current politics in depth for hours.

Sworn evidence is produced to counter new revelations and cross examinations are conducted to attack the credibility of the parties who swore the affidavits.

In the example at hand, one sister is battling one brother. It is likely that the other daughter will be drawn into the fray to support either her sister or her brother. She is likely to be forced into a position where she will alienate either her sister or her brother. Through the process, the saddest element is that a family is being destroyed.

Evidence to prove capacity or incapacity can involve many parties. Often professionals are called as witnesses. For example, the brother may call as a witness the lawyer and his staff who took the instructions from Dad and who witnessed him signing the Will. The sister may want to use the evidence of Dad's doctors who treated him to show that Dad was not mentally capable. The range of evidence is broad. The exercise of gathering evidence might encompass everyone who touched the life of the Will-maker immediately before, during and after the time of the preparation of the Will. The evidence of the professionals is important. However, in many cases, evidence of Dad's everyday conduct from people such as friends, bank tellers and storekeepers, who dealt with him, is just as important.

Where a conflict does take this form, it is not remotely like in a one-hour TV show or a two-and-a-half hour movie. The battle is often lengthy, bitter and prohibitively expensive both financially and in the destructive effect it can have on the family.

b)   Undue Influence

A valid Will expresses the intention of the person making it. The contents of the Will must not be the result of threats, force or what the law describes as "undue influence."

Clearly, a Will that is proven to be the result of the Will-maker being threatened with physical harm is not valid. What is not so easy to determine, however, are certain situations that involve more subtle coercive acts.

To illustrate situations such as this, let us look at the following example:

Father is a widower living alone in the same city as his daughter. His only other child is his son, who lives in another part of the country. Father has always loved both of his children equally. His feelings find expression in his Will, which divides all he has equally between both of his children. His children are cool to one another through no fault of Father.

Although Father is mentally competent, he is elderly and for the last several years, has increasingly relied on his daughter to help him with various chores and for companionship. He cannot rely on his son for help and personal companionship because the son lives so far away.

Father's eyesight begins to degrade and as a consequence he must give up driving. Because of the daughter's employment, she cannot drive him around during business hours. She suggests to him that he take taxis, but his feelings are hurt. She agrees to accommodate him by reducing her hours at work, provided that he compensates her. Father tells her that he wants to treat both of his children equally, but she insists on this compensation, particularly reminding him of what she has already been doing for him over the last few years.

Somewhat reluctantly, he agrees and the daughter prepares an amendment to the Will, giving her a gift of $80,000. With this gift in place, she agrees to do what Father has asked her to do for the remainder of his years.

Father dies several months later. When his son comes to learn of the gift of $80,000, he calls his sister. He expresses shock that the equal division of Dad's estate has been changed by including the extra gift to her in his Will. He accuses his sister of "putting a gun to Dad's head."

She responds that the gift expressed Dad's intention to compensate her. Dad wanted to reward her for looking after him for all the years that had gone by, and for the many years that he expected her to continue to structure her life around his wellbeing. Her brother is unconvinced, particularly because the Will was changed less than six months before Dad died. He threatens to call his lawyer to bring proceedings to declare the Will invalid if she does not renounce the $80,000 gift.

Was there sufficient undue influence to have Dad's Will declared invalid?

This is a borderline case. Of the various types of Will challenges that can be brought, undue influence is one of the most difficult to prove.

Influence, the courts say, is not enough to invalidate the Will. The influence must be of sufficient weight to qualify as *undue* influence, in order for the Will to be declared invalid. Slight coercion, promises or even persuasion are not usually enough to invalidate a Will. A judge will have to be shown that the contents of the Will did not reflect the intention of the Will-maker. The court must be satisfied that the Will-maker, if he or she could give evidence, would say, "That is not what I wanted to do, but I had to."

A major factor in determining whether there is undue influence is the vulnerability of the Will-maker. Age, illness, decreased mental ability, and dependency are all components of proving undue influence. One major factor is whether the influencer was keeping the Will-maker isolated and away from other family members or friends.

What makes undue influence even more difficult to prove is that, in most jurisdictions, the person who alleges that the Will was made because of undue influence is the one who bears the burden of proving it.

c)   Improper Signing

In order to best explain this type of challenge, we must distinguish between two types of Wills.

i)   Holograph Will

One type of Will does not require witnesses. This type of Will must be handwritten by the Will-maker and be signed by him or her. Many jurisdictions recognize this document as a legal Will. It is often referred to as a "holograph Will."

A holograph Will may be more vulnerable to a challenge because there are no witnesses to provide evidence that the Will was actually

handwritten and signed by the Will-maker. Additionally, there are
no eye witnesses to provide evidence of other crucial matters, such
as the mental capacity of the Will-maker at the time the Will was
signed. Accordingly, holograph Wills are more easily subject to
challenges based on forgery and incapacity, than formal Wills
prepared by a lawyer.

A brief story will illustrate how serious a challenge of this nature can
be. In his Will, a business owner left his business to his son, who had
operated it for years. The rest of his estate was equally divided
between that son and a daughter. All of this was expressed in a
properly prepared and witnessed Will.

However, in his formal Will, the father failed to mention a valuable
piece of land which was part of the business operation. The father
did not discover his oversight until shortly before his death. He
sought to remedy this oversight by preparing a holograph
amendment to his Will. This, he hoped, would ensure that his son
would have the full benefit of the business and the land it was on.

After Dad died, the daughter attacked the holograph amendment,
claiming that her brother had forged Dad's handwriting and
signature. She fought her brother over the question of the valuable
piece of property mentioned in the challenged holograph document.
Because there were no witnesses to confirm the validity of Dad's
handwriting and signature, the case dragged on for years.

The case was eventually settled, but it cost both parties a significant
amount of money and ended any relationship between Dad's only
two children. If Dad had made a formal amendment to his Will that
involved witnesses, perhaps the fight could have been avoided.

When an executor is faced with an estate to be administered in
accordance with a holograph Will, that executor will often be taking
steps to find evidence to prove the handwriting and signature on
that Will. Often such steps will take the executor to the offices of the
bank or other financial institution that dealt with the Will-maker.
The executor will hope for some form of verification of the signature
by comparison to signature cards and bank documents kept in the

bank's records. If the holograph Will is challenged, the parties will need to hire handwriting experts to investigate the signature and handwriting.

In the case of an elderly or infirm person, his or her signature may change as his or her strength and muscular motor skills deteriorate. The signature on the holograph Will may no longer match a signature that in the past was recognizable. The signatures on file with the bank or financial institution may not be helpful in this situation.

From our experience, there can be serious problems when a Will-maker chooses to make a holograph Will.

ii)   Formal Wills

We turn now to the subject of a formal Will, which requires that the Will-maker sign it in front of two or more witnesses. A formal Will is far more likely than a holograph Will to avoid the problems associated with a deteriorating signature.

However, having said that, there remain other challenges that arise even in the case of a formal Will. For example, in most jurisdictions the law requires that a formal Will be signed by the Will-maker, with all witnesses being present at the time of signing. The witnesses must also sign the Will in front of each other and the Will-maker.

While on the surface this may sound simple, take the case of a person who left $100,000 to a charity, in her formal Will, thereby infuriating her only son, who expected to get her entire estate. He retained an investigator to interview the witnesses. The investigator reported that while one of the witnesses was present when the Will-maker signed the Will, the other one came in after the first witness left and witnessed the Will. Based on this report, the son was successfully able to attack the validity of that Will. Because the Will was found to be invalid and because she had no prior Will, his mother was declared to have died without a Will. This entitled the son to his mother's entire estate.

Many issues can arise regarding the signing and witnessing of Wills. For example, there are restrictions on who can witness a Will. In some cases, an improper witness may invalidate the Will completely. In other cases, it may only invalidate a portion of the Will, but not the whole Will. For example, where a beneficiary who is named in a Will is also a witness, that beneficiary may lose his entitlement under the Will. However, the rest of the Will may still be valid.

In many jurisdictions, the formalities of witnessing a Will are relaxed under certain circumstances. Depending on where you live, a court can allow a Will to be valid, even if the signing or witnessing of it does not strictly comply with the rules regarding the making of formal Wills.

Sometimes, Will-makers are unable to make a full signature, either because of physical difficulties, illiteracy, blindness or language barriers. In many areas, courts will recognize the use of an "X" or other mark on the page to represent the signature.

d) The Will was Revoked before Death

An otherwise perfectly valid Will may not be effective to distribute the estate if it was revoked or cancelled before the Will-maker died. Assuming the Will-maker has mental capacity, he or she can revoke or cancel his Will at any time before he or she dies. Even if the Will was valid at one time, the issue becomes whether the Will-maker revoked that Will before he or she died.

Revocation of a Will can occur in two ways:

1. intentionally by the Will-maker, for example, by making a new Will or destroying the old one; or

2. in some jurisdictions, automatically, by the Will-maker getting married after making the Will.

If the Will is found to have been revoked, all of the beneficiaries named in that Will lose their entitlements. Therefore, there can be a dispute over whether a Will was legally revoked before death

A Will-maker who wishes to revoke or cancel his or her Will has a number of options.

If he or she makes a completely new Will, in most cases, that new Will cancels the previous Will. If he or she doesn't wish to make a new Will, but merely to revoke the current one, he or she may either physically destroy the Will or formally declare in writing his or her intention to revoke it.

There are numerous cases dealing with whether a Will has been "destroyed." Some examples of actual cases involve a Will that was only partially torn, or where a part of the Will was cut out, or even where the Will-maker's signature was cut out.

It should also be noted that in most cases, if the Will-maker just writes the words "Revoked" or "Cancelled" across the Will, this may not, in law, void the Will.

In some jurisdictions, a perfectly valid Will may be automatically revoked by the simple fact of the Will-maker getting married after the Will was made. In some cases, questions may be raised as to the validity of the marriage, since only a valid marriage revokes a Will.

Here's an example:

John is a widower whose Will leaves his entire estate to his adult children, now that his wife has passed away. John subsequently marries Susan, and in the jurisdiction in which John lives, the law provides that his marriage to Susan revokes that Will. John does not realize that the law has this effect, and believes that his children are protected under the terms of his Will. He does not make a new Will after his marriage to Susan. Suddenly and unexpectedly, John dies in an accident. Susan claims that her marriage to John revoked his Will. Because he did not make any other Will, he is deemed to have died without a Will. Susan, as his spouse, claims she is automatically entitled to a significant part of his estate because he died without a Will. John's children will not get his entire estate, as provided for in John's Will, if John is found to have died without a Will.

One of the children discovers that if he can find a way to invalidate his dad's marriage to Susan, then Dad's Will will still be valid. The children retain a lawyer to challenge Dad's marriage to Susan. If a court finds the marriage to be invalid, then the Will that gave everything to John's children is still effective.

Marriages can be challenged just as Wills can be challenged. However, challenging a marriage is usually more difficult than challenging a Will. The measure of capacity to marry is a milder test than the test of capacity to make a Will. In other words, a person can have insufficient capacity to make a Will and yet have sufficient capacity to marry.

One form of challenge to a marriage is proof that one of the parties did not have sufficient mental capacity to form an intention to marry. If proven, the marriage will be found to be invalid by a lack of consent. Another form of challenge is proof of undue influence or proof that one of the parties was substantially misled to the point that he or she was "tricked" into the marriage.

e)   A Successful Will Challenge - What Happens?

We have now seen several avenues of attack, which if successful lead to a court declaration that the Will is invalid. We examined attacks based on the lack of mental capacity, undue influence, improper signing and revocation. Before an attack of this nature is commenced, there are certain facts of life that the attacker must carefully consider. Otherwise, the attack may backfire.

What if the attack is successful?

If the Will-maker had a previous Will, that previous Will becomes the last Will of the deceased, and that Will is the one that governs the estate.

If there was no such previous Will, the deceased will be found to have died without a Will. The law that governs the scheme of distribution where there is no Will varies from jurisdiction to jurisdiction. The law is usually very strict as to who will inherit an estate with no Will. For example, in some jurisdictions, a spouse who had been separated from the deceased for many years is still entitled to a share of his or her estate if he or she dies without a Will. On the other hand, a long-time common law spouse may not be recognized as an heir, while a spouse who legally married the deceased would be entitled even if that marriage lasted only a day. Children who are devoted caregivers will be treated the same way as alienated and hostile children who have not exchanged a word with the deceased for many years.

In some jurisdictions, any relatives, however distant, are entitled to inherit before the estate becomes government property.

The following is an example of the distribution of an estate without a Will in one jurisdiction:

If the deceased died leaving a spouse, but no children, the spouse takes the entire estate. If there is one child, the spouse will receive the first $200,000 of estate assets and will share the rest equally with that child. If there are two or more children, the rest of the estate (after the first $200,000 is given to the spouse) is divided 1/3 to the spouse and the rest to the children equally. In this particular jurisdiction, the definition of "child" excludes a step child, but includes an adopted child and an "illegitimate" child.

In the jurisdiction we are discussing,

- if the deceased dies without a spouse or children, the parents take the estate;

- if there are no parents, the estate is equally divided among the siblings of the deceased.

- if a sibling dies, his share will be allocated among his own children, if he has any and if he has none, then the remaining siblings will divide the estate equally among themselves.

- if there are no siblings and no children of siblings, then the next link in the chain will include cousins. The links in this chain follow blood lines until it can be established that there is no living relative.

The above examples are taken from one jurisdiction. As inheritance laws vary from place to place, the pattern of distribution will also vary. As a result, it would be wise to check with your own lawyer to determine the applicable law in your own case.

Considering the above information, it is evident that any party who considers attacking a Will must consider where he or she will stand, from the point of view of inheritance, if his or her challenge is successful. There are some examples of ill-conceived challenges, which might help to illustrate this point.

Imagine a common law couple living in a jurisdiction that does not recognize the rights of inheritance of a common law partner where the partner dies without a Will. Imagine that in such a case, the man dies, leaving his common law spouse $100,000 in his Will, which represents only a small portion of his estate. To the common law spouse, this is a slap in the face. In her fury, she threatens an attack on the Will, and risks creating bad feelings among the rest of the family.

It is only when she receives sobering advice from her lawyer that she relents in her hostility. He explains to her that if she does succeed in setting aside the Will she will lose the $100,000 gift in the Will. The result of a successful Will challenge is that her common law spouse will be deemed to have died without a Will. The lawyer explains that the applicable law provides no inheritance rights to a common law spouse where there is no Will. She gains no benefit from challenging the Will. In fact, a Will challenge would backfire, costing her the $100,000 gift.

He advises her to focus on negotiation with the family.

This example serves to illustrate that before tempers flare and fragile relationships are shattered, it is critically important to have a grasp of where one stands in terms of inheritance rights, if successful in a Will challenge.

Here is another example:

Mr. Smith owned a factory. After his wife died, he was left with his two children. His son, a very hard worker, joined him in the business after college. Mr. Smith prepared a Will, leaving his entire business to his son, and the balance of the estate equally between his son and daughter. That Will was kept by his lawyer, who held it for many years. Neither of his children knew of this Will. Over time, the business expanded, Mr. Smith changed lawyers and now both children were in the business with Mr. Smith. Mr. Smith recognized that his son was contributing far more to the business than his daughter, even though both were drawing the same salary.

Because his daughter was now in the business, Mr. Smith wanted to make a new Will. In the new Will he left 70% of the business to his son and 30% to his daughter. When Mr. Smith died, and the Will was disclosed to his children, his daughter was furious at only receiving 30% of the business. She immediately consulted a lawyer. Not knowing about Mr. Smith's first Will, which left 100% of the business to his son, the lawyer explained that if the Will that left her 30% of the business was found invalid, her father would be deemed to have died without a Will. Consequently, she and her brother would be treated equally.

She thought she had found a way to attack the manner in which the Will was signed, after employees of the company told her that her brother was putting pressure on her father. The lawyer had told her that undue influence exerted by her brother on her father, inducing her father to change his Will, might lead to a court finding the Will invalid.

In preparing for the court hearing, the brother located the first Will. You can only imagine the surprise of the daughter when she learned of the first Will, and its gift of the entire business to her brother. It became very clear that her efforts to seek a victory in court brought no benefit to her. The provisions in the first Will gave her brother a greater benefit than the one which she was trying to take away from him under the new Will.

The moral of this story is that it is dangerous to initiate a challenge to the validity of a Will in a vacuum. The course of proceedings may yield very unwelcome and unexpected surprises. You must always know what will happen if you "win" the Will challenge.

2. CLAIMS AGAINST THE ESTATE

It is important to recognize that not all estate litigation raises the issue of the validity of a Will. In the last section, we examined Will challenges. Now we will examine other claims that do not call into question the validity of the Will, but may still effect the distribution of the estate.

a) Spousal Claims

Imagine that your husband dies and you find out that in his Will he left everything to the children of his first marriage. The lawyer representing his children demands possession of the house you are living in. You feel that you are on the verge of being homeless and dispossessed of almost everything you shared with your husband. Can the law really be that harsh? You can take some comfort from this:

A spouse enjoys the protection of the law in almost every jurisdiction. Such protection varies from place to place. However, the law generally does not permit one spouse to completely disinherit the other. Most jurisdictions entitle a surviving spouse to what the law considers a "fair share" of the estate.

In some jurisdictions, the law allows a spouse to elect for a share of the deceased spouse's estate instead of accepting what the Will provides for. In other jurisdictions, spouses are required to share all property on death. Still other jurisdictions provide for the right of the spouse to continue to live in the matrimonial home, or for ongoing financial support.

Let's examine how a spousal election against the Will affects the distribution of an estate in one particular jurisdiction. The following example illustrates what happens if a surviving spouse chooses to exercise his or her right, rather than taking what was provided under the Will.

Suppose a husband's Will leaves his wife $2,000.00 per month for the rest of her life. His Will requires that the capital of the estate be held in trust for the rest of the wife's life, and that the children would receive what is left of that capital only after the wife passes away.

The wife will have to decide whether to accept the $2,000 per month or to "elect" to receive whatever lump sum amount is prescribed by law.

The election might have a beneficial effect for both her *and* the children, even though it is not what her husband intended. By electing for her share, she gets a lump sum right away and the children also receive the balance of the estate right away, instead of having to wait for their share until after the wife's death. Of course, the children's share will be reduced by the amount that the wife receives as part of her lump sum.

The law that governs marital property is complex and requires specific legal advice. For example, the right of a spouse to elect for a share of the estate must be exercised within strict time limits.
There are further factors to consider as well, such as the provisions of pre-nuptial agreements and the rights of partners in common law and same-sex relationships.

b)   Dependant's Support Claims

Most jurisdictions require Will-makers, after their deaths, to provide ongoing support to their surviving dependants. If that support is not specified in the Will, the courts in most areas will order support out of the estate to be paid to those "dependants."

This type of claim is only open to those who fall under the definition of "dependant." This is one area of the law where a particular claim might be valid in one jurisdiction yet a similar claim might fail in a different jurisdiction. However, generally speaking, close family members have rights to support from the deceased's estate where they were receiving "support" or were entitled to support from the deceased before he or she died. Depending on the jurisdiction, the definition of "support" can be very broad. For example, if Dad was allowing one of his adult children to live with him in his home rent-free or at a reduced rent, this might be considered to be "support" to that child.

The definition of "dependants," in some jurisdictions, includes both minor and adult children, grandchildren, parents, siblings, spouses, common law partners and same-sex partners.

Imagine a father whose wife passed away, leaving him to care for his two young children. Dad meets another woman, and in the course of their relationship, Dad makes a new Will. The Will leaves everything to her. Unexpectedly, Dad passes away. His children, who are completing high school, find out that there has been no provision made for them in Dad's Will. They also know that Dad's new wife has little interest in them. Understandably, they are concerned about how they will be supported and who will pay for their college education.

Most jurisdictions give those children the right to be supported from Dad's estate, because before Dad died he was supporting those children. In those jurisdictions, the children would be able to claim support from Dad's estate, regardless of what Dad's Will says.

Wills that contain token gifts to dependants in the hope that no further money will be paid to these dependants out of the estate do not always work. In many cases, the courts hold that the token gifts do not disqualify the dependants from getting the support to which the law entitles them.

Where a claim is made by a dependant, a court will determine what support should be paid from the estate. Not all dependant claims are accepted by the court. The type of support that a court can grant is flexible. If the situation merits it, the award might be very specific, such as the right to live in a particular residence for a number of years, or even for the life of the claimant. A court judgment might go even further, forcing the estate to give a piece of real estate, such as a family home, to the claimant.

The court has the power to force the estate to pay money to the claimant, either in a lump sum or in instalments on an ongoing basis.

There are circumstances in which the deceased may have been under a Court Order to pay alimony or support to a spouse or a child during his or her lifetime. It is likely that that spouse or child would be considered a dependant. The amount of such payments may be varied by a judge after death. This may occur if that judge decides that the level of support set out in the old Court Order is no longer adequate under the circumstances occurring after the death of the deceased. In some jurisdictions, the court can even override provisions and limitations contained in separation agreements, domestic agreements, or pre-nuptial agreements.

c)   **Compensation for Services**

Imagine that over a period of years, you have been a dutiful and helpful son to your elderly mother. Although you don't live with her, you take three afternoons out of your busy week to look after many of her needs. Although you make this sacrifice, none of your siblings makes any effort to help Mom out. You never complain when you have to clear the snow from her driveway or take off extra time so that you can be there when the roofer or the plumber has to be told what to do. You take her garbage out. You drive Mom to the doctor and dentist and wait for her for hours, reading magazines in the waiting room while she is being looked after.

Mom's Will splits all that she had equally between you and your two siblings. To your surprise, her Will is silent as to any reward or recognition for fifteen years of sacrifice on your part. When, a month after her death, you mildly suggest to your siblings that Mom intended to compensate you, your sister reacts, telling you, "No way! Mom's Will leaves everything equally and that's how she wanted it!"

Is that the end of it or do you have any other options?

The law may recognize your efforts and order compensation to you from the estate.

To begin with, the court will need proof that you provided valuable services to the deceased during her lifetime. Secondly, you must show that you never got paid or compensated in any way for these services.

Assuming that this has been proven, the next important issue is the relationship the claimant had to the deceased. For example, if the claimant was a friend and not a child, the law would more likely recognize that compensation should be paid for these services. The law would not assume that a friend provides free services out of love. However, because you are a son, in order to be able to succeed in your claim, you must be able to prove that there was more to the relationship than just a son performing the services out of love for his mother.

Every claimant will say that he or she expected to be paid for those services. However, that is not enough. To be entitled to compensation, you must show more than your own expectation that you were to be given something. You must prove to the court that the deceased also intended that you would be compensated.

What makes this an uphill battle for you is the fact that Mom is not there to speak. You must prove that Mom intended you to be compensated. To do this, you need what the law calls "corroboration." Essentially, "corroboration" is credible evidence coming from someone other than from you, which supports your argument. An example would be a letter from Mom expressing her intention that you be paid. A court might also consider verbal evidence from credible witnesses, such as friends or other family members.

Here are two different examples of this type of claim:

The deceased verbally promises to transfer her house or other asset to the caregiver when she dies, if the caregiver looks after her for the rest of her life. When she dies, her Will does not make any reference to this arrangement. The caregiver asserts a claim to the asset he was promised, and meets resistance from those who benefit under the Will. To succeed, the caregiver must be able to prove the promise, and that he fulfilled his end of the bargain.

The court is looking for proof of an arrangement between the deceased and the caregiver, which was understood and agreed to by both parties.

The other example involves an elderly woman's companion, who visits her often and spends a great deal of time with her. He is a great help to her because he cuts her lawn and paints her house. He even did all the work to renovate her home by fixing up the basement and putting in a new shower. His work increased the value of her home. She never paid him for doing the work. When she dies she leaves that home to her children. The children inherit a property that is worth much more because of the companion's work. He is surprised that her Will leaves him nothing to compensate for all that he has done. Why should her children get more because of his hard work? This is the question that the court will ask itself if he brings a claim against the estate. If the court feels that the children would be unjustly enriched as a result of the companion's hard work, it may award him compensation from the estate or even a portion of the house.

d)   Challenges to Gifts made during Life

Gifts made by the deceased during his or her lifetime are not immune from estate litigation. In certain situations, a beneficiary, or the estate, may challenge those gifts arguing that their value should fall into the estate for distribution under the Will.

To illustrate a challenge of this nature:

You are one of four children. Your brother lives in the same city with Dad. You and your two sisters live in different cities.

Although Dad was in his eighties, he seemed to you and your two sisters to be functioning independently when you saw him at Christmas and birthdays.

A few weeks ago Dad died. Dad's Will left everything equally among the four of you. Although Dad rarely talked about money, it was evident that he was fairly well off, owning his own house, a bank account, a retirement fund and investments. Knowing what Mom had when she died, you figure that your portion of Dad's estate would be approximately $200,000.

You are shocked when you read the letter from the lawyer for the estate. He says that when Dad died, his estate was only $120,000 in total. It seems impossible that the estate could be so small. Yet the lawyer explains why.

Dad had changed the ownership papers to his house so that he held it jointly with your brother. He also explains that your dad gifted most of his investments to your brother a year before he died. Similarly, he named your brother as sole beneficiary of his retirement fund.

The lawyer explains that Dad's Will was only effective to divide what Dad owned when he died. The lawyer further explains that joint ownership means that upon Dad's death, the surviving joint owner automatically takes the entire asset. Therefore, Dad's Will does not apply to the house. The house automatically goes to your brother, as the surviving joint owner. The lawyer also advises that under the laws of that jurisdiction, the retirement fund passes outside of Dad's estate to your brother because he is designated as the sole beneficiary.

Similarly, Dad's Will cannot distribute assets that Dad gave away during his lifetime, like the investments.

The question posed by the three of you is:

Can these "gifts" by Dad to your brother be challenged so that they are brought back into Dad's estate to be distributed according to Dad's Will?

The lawyer explains that the answer depends on:

- whether Dad really intended to give your brother all of those assets as genuine gifts;

- whether Dad had placed the assets in your brother's name to make it more convenient for your brother to help Dad manage his finances; and

- whether Dad was mentally incapable or unduly influenced by your brother to make these transfers to him.

Considering that the question involves over $750,000, the three of you decide to retain a lawyer to look into the matter. The lawyer retains a private investigator and after a month the three of you meet again with your lawyer. At that meeting, you recall how Dad had explained, learning from a newspaper article, that he could save probate fees by holding assets jointly. Your lawyer notes this at the meeting. Then the lawyer explains what the private investigator found:

- Dad went to your brother's lawyer a few days before he died and transferred the house into joint names with your brother. The lawyer has no notes of his meeting with your dad.

- One of Dad's friends told the investigator that Dad was always complaining that three of the kids were never around. However, the same friend also said that your brother appeared to be a very controlling individual.

- According to the bank manager, your brother was helping Dad manage his investments. However, the bank manager recounted a conversation with Dad where he complained about your brother not keeping him informed about his assets.

Stepping back from this narrative, some issues arise.

First of all, just how hard will it be for these deprived beneficiaries to successfully unwind these transfers of money and property?

The brother has title documents that clearly show his name as owner of the assets. His lawyer states that Dad made these gifts to him during his lifetime and that is the end of the story. The brother's lawyer will rely on the legal assumption that a person can do whatever he wants with his property while he is alive. Depending on where you live, a transfer of assets from a parent to a child may be automatically presumed to be intended as a gift, unless there is evidence to show that a gift was *not* intended.

The siblings will argue that Dad did not intend the transfers to be gifts. They will try to bring enough evidence to court to convince a judge that Dad transferred the assets to the brother for a reason other than an outright gift. There are many circumstances where a parent's transfer of assets to a child is not intended as a gift to that child. For example, many elderly people want to have one of their children help them with their banking. As a result, they may decide to put a child's name on the bank account. Similarly, a parent may re-arrange the ownership of his assets to minimize tax owing on his death. In each of these cases, the parent's intention is not to give away ownership to the child.

Dad must have sufficient mental capacity to make valid gifts to the brother. If the siblings can show that Dad did not understand what he was doing when he transferred the assets to the brother, the gifts will not be valid.

If the court finds that Dad did not intend the transfers to be gifts or that Dad did not have the mental capacity to make the gifts, the assets transferred by Dad to the brother will have to be transferred back to the estate. They will then be divided among the beneficiaries of the Will.

As you can tell, there are risks when gifts are made to one child during a parent's lifetime to the exclusion of the other children. How do you protect yourself as a recipient of a gift, or as a parent who wishes to make a legitimate gift to one of your children?

The answer lies in a clear written expression of intention to make the gift.

If the person who made the gift to you has already passed away and you are under attack, it would be helpful if you could find a letter written by the deceased, which indicates that he intended to give this particular asset to you as a gift.

Assume that you, as a parent, wish to gift an asset to your child during your lifetime either by an outright transfer or making him a joint owner, you should consider the following:

In addition to the formal documents that are necessary to transfer the asset to the child's name, you should also document your intention. This may mean preparing a letter that specifically identifies that asset and states your intention to give this asset to him as a gift. You should sign and date that letter. You should also consider having a lawyer document your intention. The lawyer can also confirm that you are of sound mind and free from undue influence from your child. This will go a long way toward protecting the recipient from attack from a beneficiary under your Will who claims that the gift was not really a gift.

e)   Abuse Claims

We have examined various types of claims against an estate, all of which may be possible even where the claimant was entirely cut out of the Will.

Another example of such a claim involves circumstances where the deceased is found to have physically, emotionally or sexually abused a person.

If a court finds that the deceased abused the claimant, he or she may be entitled to get damages from the estate to compensate for the abuse. These damages would come out of the estate and would be paid to the abused person before the beneficiaries in the Will receive anything from the estate.

To succeed in such a claim, the person who suffered the abuse must prove to the court that he or she suffered physical, emotional or sexual abuse from the deceased.

Claims of this nature are often complicated by the passage of time since the abuse occurred. Firstly, because the deceased is not alive to defend him or herself, the law generally requires that such claims be supported by independent evidence. Medical records are often the best evidence of such claims.

Secondly, there may be concerns over the limitation period for bringing the claim. Every jurisdiction is subject to legislation that allows a claimant only so many years in which to sue. Once the number of years specified in the statute of limitations has passed, the claimant no longer can succeed in his lawsuit because he or she waited too long to start it. In cases of abuse, the law may still preserve the rights of the abused person to sue, even after the time specified in the statute of limitations has passed.

For example:

A child sued his father's estate on the grounds of the father's physical abuse when the child was young. Over 40 years had passed between the occurrence of the abusive acts and the commencement of the lawsuit. The court awarded the claimant a portion of the estate of his abusive father, even though he was cut out of the Will. The court found that, because of the abuse, the claimant was psychologically unable to make a claim against his father until the father died. Therefore, the court started the limitation period only when the father died, and the claimant was psychologically able to confront the abuse. Because of the extension of the limitation period, the lawsuit was permitted to go forward.

The other problem faced by this claimant was that of providing independent evidence of the abuse. The claimant was able to provide hospital records to prove to the court that he was abused. He had been admitted to hospital several times when he was a child. The experts were able to convince the court that those injuries resulted from the father's abuse.

3. CLAIMS INVOLVING THE EXECUTOR

As we have seen previously, the executor may face challenges from the beneficiaries relating to his or her administration of the estate. Executors are responsible to the beneficiaries to ensure that they fulfill their duties in administering the estate. Beneficiaries will often keep a close eye on what the executor is doing for this reason: every dollar that is paid out or lost by the executor reduces the amount the beneficiaries will get from the estate.

The executor has certain duties and the beneficiaries have corresponding rights. As you read this, you may be a beneficiary or an executor. This section will address both the duties and the rights. By reading this, the executor will see what pitfalls to avoid and the beneficiaries will see what to do to protect their rights.

EXECUTORS BEWARE - BENEFICIARIES BE AWARE

a)   Ten Common Executor's Mistakes

Here are 10 of the most common mistakes made by executors and how they can cause a Family War between the executor and beneficiaries:

1.   Don't Do Anything - The beneficiaries will wait forever for their money.

Most beneficiaries will want their money as soon as reasonably possible.

How long should it take to administer an estate? There is no hard and fast rule on how quickly an estate must be administered. When a concerned beneficiary feels that the executor is not moving ahead quickly enough with the administration, the question of who is right or wrong is a matter of determining what is reasonable in the circumstances.

As a beneficiary, you must realize that there is a lot of work for the executor to do before distributing the money or assets to the beneficiaries. All parties are likely to understand that during the period of mourning, the executor may not turn his mind to business. However, if an executor is not up to the tasks involved after the grieving has ended, he or she should consider resigning or else face the consequences of inaction.

Strategically, the executor is prudent to delay distribution until determination of spousal claims or claims for support by dependants. Some jurisdictions allow a full year for the executor to carry out his or her distribution. When distribution does take place, it is usually a partial distribution, with the balance of the estate held back for the purpose of determining remaining liabilities for which the estate and the executor him or herself might be responsible.

Before impatience drives you, as a beneficiary, to attack your brother, who is the executor, you must realize that silence on his part does not necessarily mean inactivity. You must also realize that an attack on your brother may be interpreted as an unforgivable act, causing serious stress on your relationship with him. Imagine then how your brother might feel if he is actually hard at work on the estate, but you don't know it, and in those circumstances you attack him. Apologies may not be enough.

2.   Don't Invest Estate Money – Just leave it in a bank account.

Initially, the executor takes over whatever assets the deceased had at the time of death. Money sitting in a bank account will not generate much interest. Volatile stocks which had a very high market value when the deceased died may dwindle in value at the hands of an idle executor.

The executor must maximize the value of the estate. Leaving large amounts of money in an estate bank account with little or no interest costs the beneficiaries money. Similarly, a drop in the share price of the deceased's investments after death will also reduce the beneficiaries' slice of the pie.

Executors must act in the best interests of the beneficiaries, and must be aware that at some point they will be questioned on what they did with the assets of the estate. Beneficiaries will be understandably upset if they see that the assets were either not invested or invested in speculative investments that declined in value after death. Beneficiaries are entitled to know how estate assets were invested by the executor.

Beneficiaries should be concerned where particulars of the estate investments are being hidden from them, or where the assets are being invested unwisely by the executor.

Of course, the executor cannot be blamed for a downturn in the market, where he or she has invested in solid blue chip securities. Regardless, an executor must be prudent in his or her investment choices. Obtaining specialized advice from investment professionals is also a wise precaution.

3.   Don't File Tax Returns - Just let penalties and interest grow.

Before an executor distributes assets of an estate to the beneficiaries, he or she must clear all debts and taxes legitimately owed by the estate. In order to clear debts and taxes, he or she must know what they are. This requires careful investigation by the executor.

Part of this process must involve ensuring that all the deceased's and the estate's tax returns and filings have been submitted to the government. If all is in order, the government approves the tax submissions and filings. A prudent executor will usually retain the services of an accountant, who is familiar with these matters, for the purpose of fulfilling these functions. Although the cost of an accountant is usually paid by the estate, this expense is often a wise investment. Tax professionals can benefit the estate by avoiding needless interest and penalties and by taking advantage of various tax exemptions with which the executor may not be familiar.

The executor must be very careful. If he or she underestimates the outstanding tax owing and distributes assets of the estate that should have been used to satisfy the estate's tax obligations, the executor will be at personal financial risk to the government. If the executor ignores the tax liabilities, and as a result the estate erodes because of excessive interest and penalties, then the executor could be exposed to a lawsuit from disgruntled beneficiaries.

Beneficiaries should request copies of the tax returns filed by the executor or other documents that will confirm that the estate did not incur penalties or interest for late tax filings.

4.   Don't Check for Creditors – Let the creditors sue you after distribution.

This risk is similar to the one we have just mentioned regarding taxes, but there are some distinctions that arise. It is generally easy to confirm what the deceased owed for taxes by contacting the government. However, where a private creditor emerges after the death of a person, the executor must be alert.

There is always the possibility that an illegitimate claim against the estate will surface. The executor must be cautious and must do all that a reasonable person can do to determine the authenticity of such a claim before paying it.

For example, the deceased before he died, may have entered into a contract to have his roof repaired. A few months after death, the roofer produces the contract and claims that the deceased never paid for the work. While you confirm that the deceased did not pay for the work, there may have been good reason not to do so. Perhaps the work was shoddy or not fully completed. In such a case, if the executor paid the claim in full, he could be liable to the beneficiaries.

On the other hand, the executor may also face the personal risk of a lawsuit brought by a legitimate unpaid creditor. If the executor distributes assets of the estate to beneficiaries without leaving enough in the estate to pay for the legitimate creditor, the executor may be personally liable to pay the claim. As we have seen, to protect him or herself, the executor should advertise for creditors of the estate.

If the estate does not pay its legitimate claimants, these claimants may be able to go after the beneficiaries to the extent of what the beneficiaries inherited. Concerned beneficiaries should inquire about any claims paid by the executor to ensure that they were legitimate. Having said that, in many jurisdictions executors are given broad discretion to settle any claims as long as the settlement or payment of the claim is done in good faith.

5. Pay All Lawyer's and Accountant's Bills Without Checking Them - The beneficiaries won't care that you have spent their money unwisely.

The prudent executor depends heavily on proper legal and accounting representation for the estate. As long as the services were necessary and reasonably priced, he or she would not normally be facing the risk of a lawsuit by beneficiaries.

There are times when unexpected events occur in an estate administration that result in higher professional fees. Such fees are not usually problematic when the appropriate explanations clarify the reasons for the excess time and effort that had to be expended. However, the executor must be cautious in paying accounts that are disproportionately high, well beyond the estimates that the professional had quoted, or without appropriate explanation for such increase. In such circumstances the executor may be forced to challenge such accounts, in order to protect him or herself from being sued at a later point by one or more beneficiaries.

If you, as beneficiary, are concerned about a professional's bill, such as that of an accountant or lawyer, being paid from the estate, you should consider doing the following:

- obtain a copy of the bill;

- ensure that the services rendered by the professional are detailed in the account;

- consult with your own lawyer or accountant to determine whether the fees charged are in the normal range of what could be expected for the work performed; and

- review the work performed to ensure that the services provided were truly the professional's work and not the *executor's* work. For example, if the lawyer charged the estate for depositing money into the estate account, this would be work the executor is responsible to do. Any fees paid to the lawyer for doing executor's work should generally be deducted from the amount of the executor's compensation to be paid to the executor.

6.   Don't Keep an Accounting - Everyone will trust you.

One of the essential obligations of an executor is the obligation to account for the estate assets.

The accounting must encompass every asset in the estate, and every asset entering and leaving the estate, whether in monetary form or otherwise. The executor must maintain his or her accounts on an ongoing basis, so that he or she is ready with those accounts on very short notice.

Here is an example of a failure to account:

Imagine that the executor has expended hundreds or perhaps thousands of dollars of estate money, for various purposes. Because he or she has not kept accurate records, he or she cannot explain where the money has gone.

In his or her explanation to the beneficiaries, he or she can only state that these were "miscellaneous expenses." An entry of that nature will encourage suspicion by beneficiaries and erode the credibility of the executor in their eyes.

With a view to understanding the gravity of this executor's obligation, let us examine his or her duty to account, through the eyes of the beneficiaries.

How can a Beneficiary force an executor to account?

Demands for accounting can often be a trigger for an all-out Family War. Failure to provide a regular accounting creates suspicion. However, as soon as one is demanded, it often causes hurt, affront and defensiveness. "Don't you trust me?" is what executors often say when the beneficiaries demand an accounting. The beneficiaries must bear in mind that, depending on how the demands are made, their relationship with their executor-sibling may be damaged for years, well beyond the end of the administration of the estate.

Two sisters may be looking for answers from their brother, who is sole executor. We would suggest that they try at the outset to tread more lightly than a typical litigant might. The beneficiaries must recognize that it can take time to compile an accurate accounting. If the beneficiaries have heard nothing from the executor for some time, it may be necessary to start taking some steps.

Instead of immediately having your lawyer send a letter, the beneficiaries might consider, as a first step, calling their executor-brother and asking in a non-confrontational manner for an accounting.

Assuming that their verbal request yields no success, then they would, as a next step, write to their executor-brother requesting a status report and accounting from him. They would ask in their letter that he account for all funds received, disbursed and invested. They would ask for a response within a time limit, and the time limit would be reasonable. They should also suggest that if the time limit is not feasible, to have the executor suggest one. Their letter at this point should not be accusatory or threatening. They might at the same time tell their brother that they would appreciate a regular accounting. A firm but non-accusatory demand from the sisters at this stage will hopefully avoid animosity.

If the reasonable time period that they specified in their letter has elapsed without a response from their brother, they would write another letter providing one last extension to him. This, hopefully, will make it clear to their brother that they mean business. They would now let him know that they intend to follow this letter up through a lawyer, if an answer is not forthcoming. The executor-brother should develop the clear impression from this second letter that the two requests for accounting which he has now received from his sisters are just the beginning of a paper trail that may ultimately end up before a judge. For this reason, email notices, while acceptable, are not necessarily the most effective means of communicating with the executor. Email might leave it open for the executor to argue that he did not receive the message due to some computer problem. A registered letter leaves no question that the executor received your letter.

If despite this letter the executor fails to respond, then the lawyer for the sisters will likely follow up with a letter demanding an accounting.

The lawyer may express to the executor that a failure to account will result in a court application to compel the accounting at the executor's personal expense.

The follow up to that lawyer's letter would be a court application to compel an accounting. The court will take note of the previous accounting requests and, with this paper trail in hand, the judge, in most jurisdictions, will routinely grant the order compelling the executor to account.

7. Don't Get Appraisals of Estate Assets - The beneficiaries will assume you sold at a fair price.

Executors must realize that most estate assets have a value. Executors may control such assets as personal representatives of the deceased, but executors do not own such assets. Executors face a potential financial risk in any situation where a beneficiary perceives that an estate asset has been sold for less than proper market value.

It is almost always in the best interest of an executor to obtain an appraisal of the fair market value of an estate asset before selling or disposing of it. Appraisals, when conducted for these purposes, are paid for out of estate assets. Even where an executor is facing a claim by a beneficiary for having sold an estate asset below market value, a written appraisal of the asset in question will prove to be helpful to the executor in defence of that claim.

A concerned beneficiary will request that the executor produce an appraisal for any property that was sold. This is especially the case where it was not sold on the open market, such as a sale by the executor to his or her relative or friend.

8. Give Away Property for Nothing - The beneficiaries will agree that the "antique" was really worthless.

That old table with the rusted hinges, the tattered record album covers, the dented boxes now empty, that Mom used to store her tea bags: all of these seem like candidates for a yard sale.

Perhaps your busy executor-sister can only devote a few evenings here and there to the administration of Mom's estate. She might have arranged for a dumpster so that such items and many more like them could be loaded up and carted away to the dump. The executor who assumes that these items have no value may live to regret that assumption. She risks the anger of a beneficiary who alleges that the table, the record albums and the dented tea boxes were all valuable antiques. The executor should obtain proof of the worthlessness of such items, or alternatively obtain the consent of all of the beneficiaries, in writing, to either dispose of such items or to offer them to the beneficiaries.

From the beneficiary's point of view, the executor may not appreciate that certain items have monetary value. If you are aware that the deceased owned a personal item or collection that may have value, you should immediately advise the executor of your concern.

9. Don't Communicate with the Beneficiaries - They don't care about how the administration is progressing.

The executor would be wise to communicate regularly with each of the beneficiaries on the status of the estate administration. There may be times when the process involves uncomfortably long waiting periods until the executor gets his own report from a stockbroker or a lawyer who is involved in a real estate transaction. A wise executor will consider an informal report indicating to the beneficiaries that he or she is still waiting for one thing or another, even if there is no news to report. Such contact will likely give even an anxious beneficiary a sense of comfort knowing that the executor is looking after the estate.

Where there are a number of beneficiaries, the executor should communicate directly with each beneficiary as opposed to communicating with one or more, but not all of them. Where a beneficiary receives information from his brother, who is another beneficiary, the brother who gets the information indirectly will wonder why he himself did not get the executor's report. Worse yet, where the information is important, there is a possibility that there might be miscommunication between the beneficiaries.

When the executor contacts the beneficiary, the beneficiary should not blame the executor for events which may be out of the executor's control. For example, Dad's stock certificates may have been lost by the broker, which delays the distribution; or the real estate market for Mom's house may have softened to the point where the sale price is not what everyone expected. The beneficiaries, while upset, should not blame the executor for these types of problems.

Furthermore, a beneficiary must recognize that a frustrated and unwilling executor may be permitted to step down. The beneficiary must, before levelling criticism at the executor, realize that given enough pressure, an executor might consider resigning. If that were to happen, would the beneficiary want to step in to replace that frustrated executor?

As in any conflict situation, understanding where the other side is coming from lessens the possibility of an all-out battle. To avoid problems, beneficiaries should try to understand the pressures and obligations of an executor. Similarly, the executor should try to think of how he or she would feel if he or she stood in the shoes of one of the beneficiaries. This is where experience can benefit both sides. A lawyer or other professional experienced in estate matters will quickly be able to advise the beneficiaries or executors whether or not concerns raised by the others are legitimate.

To ensure sufficient communication with the beneficiaries, some executors might wish to ask the beneficiaries how often they want to be updated.

10.   Don't Keep Track of the Time Spent Administering the Estate - Beneficiaries always agree on how much compensation the executor should get.

At the outset, an executor may be intending to fulfil his or her functions without charging compensation, out of duty or love for the deceased. Nevertheless, by the end of the administration, the executor may have been met with criticism, scepticism and lack of appreciation from beneficiaries.

Where an executor does charge compensation, the likelihood of such criticism is often heightened. An executor's written time records are usually the best evidence to show what he or she did for the estate and how much time he or she had to expend on accomplishing what he or she did.

Depending on where you live, executor's compensation is based on a number of factors, such as the size of the estate, the value and importance of the work done by the executor, and the time he or she had to spend to complete the administration. Throughout an average administration, the executor will have to expend considerable time and effort on what may appear in hindsight to the beneficiaries to be trivial issues.

For example, take the sale of the family home.

A year ago, the executor and the realtor had a dispute over the amount of real estate commission. It took over five hours of stressful telephone conversations with the realtor and the lawyer acting for the estate.

The executor's efforts may have saved the estate over $15,000 in commission. However, the beneficiaries may not recognize the efforts of the executor if nothing is presented to them to show what he or she did. The executor's journal will show all the calls made and a meeting with a lawyer at six o'clock on a Friday afternoon that lasted for over 2 hours. This will help justify the executor's claim for compensation.

The executor should keep current time records as work is done. Trying to compile a list of what you have done and how much time it took you, months or years after the event, is almost impossible. In addition, records made at the time of the event carry much more weight with a court than records made some time after.

Beneficiaries should realize that the executor is entitled to be paid reasonably for acting in the administration of the estate. His or her compensation is paid from the estate.

Sometimes one or more of the beneficiaries is insistent enough to compel court proceedings to challenge the compensation claimed by the executor. In such cases, it is possible that the estate will pay for all of the legal costs of both the executor and the challenging beneficiary. If this occurs, any reduction of executor's compensation that is achieved by the beneficiary could be off-set by the legal fees relating to the challenge, which are paid from the estate.

b)   Conflicts over Executor's Discretion

As we discussed earlier in the book, some Wills do not distribute all of the assets outright to the beneficiaries. In some cases, the assets are held in a trust for the benefit of one or more beneficiaries. Where there is a trust created in the Will, the executor is sometimes given discretion to decide when and how much a beneficiary is to receive from the estate. This is often referred to as "encroachment." An executor's decision can often lead to a dispute because the more one beneficiary receives, the less the other beneficiaries get.

The executor who is exercising his or her judgment must realize that he or she is dealing with competing interests. This balancing act can be illustrated by two examples:

1. The executor holds $250,000.00 in trust for the beneficiary until the age of 25. The executor has the right under the Will to encroach on the $250,000 for "educational purposes." The beneficiary is 18 and asks the executor for a lump sum of $15,000.00 to pay for tuition at a Yoga school. In the executor's judgment the school is not engaged in "education." The executor denies the request for the $15,000.00. The beneficiary is furious and threatens to sue the executor.

2. The executor holds $800,000 in trust for the deceased's second wife. The Will gives the executor the power to encroach upon the capital for her support. The deceased, her husband, left a letter to the executor stating that he wanted her lifestyle to be as good as it had been while they lived together. The children of the deceased, who will receive whatever is left of the $800,000 upon the second wife's death, dislike her. The executor knows that they will be watching closely to see how much encroachment occurs during the second wife's remaining life. They look upon every encroachment to the wife as a reduction of their own inheritance. She requests $65,000.00 from the estate for a luxury car. The executor agrees. The children sue the executor for misusing his or her discretion.

While these circumstances may lead to bad feelings or threats of litigation, courts will usually be reluctant to interfere with the discretion exercised by the executor. Courts will generally defer to the executor as long as the executor exercised his or her discretion reasonably and in a manner consistent with the Will.

A prudent executor will document the reasons for his or her decision to encroach or not to encroach. For example, the deceased set up a trust in his Will for his son's support until he finishes college. At age 18, the son requests that the executor encroach on the capital of his trust fund to buy a car to go to work. The executor believes that this is justified. The executor should document the son's reasons for the request and why he believes the request is justified. The executor will be able to support his decision to encroach to buy the car for the son if he is confronted by the other beneficiaries.

Consulting with a lawyer to discuss the proper considerations in making a decision is also a wise option for the executor. For example, depending on the jurisdiction, when an executor decides whether to encroach, the beneficiary's own financial situation may be relevant. In the example of the second wife, assume that she was wealthy and did not *need* the support from the estate. In some jurisdictions this may be relevant for the executor to consider, while in others it would be improper for the executor to consider her own finances in deciding how much support she should get.

c)   Removing an Executor by Court Application

If the executor is mismanaging the estate, the beneficiaries can ask the court to remove him or her and replace him or her with another executor.

However, generally speaking, in most jurisdictions, a court will be reluctant to remove an executor without a good reason. The fact that the deceased expressed confidence in the selection of that person as the executor will not be easily overturned by a court. Therefore, an executor acting in good faith, who commits minor errors, will generally not be removed by a court. However, there are situations or decisions which will motivate a court to terminate an executor. Let us examine some examples:

A.   Conflict of Interest

The court will not tolerate a situation where the personal interests of the executor are opposed to the interests of the estate. For example, if the executor owes money to the estate and is unwilling to pay it, he or she is in conflict. The interests of the estate are to collect the debt in full and the interests of the executor are to avoid paying. Theoretically, an executor who instructs a lawyer to sue on the debt would be involved on both sides of the same lawsuit and that is forbidden.

An executor selling assets to him or herself or to close friends or relatives may also be seen to be in a conflict of interest. The executor is the seller of the estate assets and has a duty to maximize their value. A buyer wants to get the assets at the lowest price possible. If the executor or someone close to him or her is the buyer and the executor, on behalf of the estate, is the seller, there is a clear conflict. Most jurisdictions will not permit an executor to purchase assets from the estate without the consent of all beneficiaries or a court order.

If the executor has to sue the estate to recover a debt owing to him or her, this too creates a conflict of interest that may result in the executor's removal. He or she cannot both sue the estate and defend the estate in the same lawsuit.

A spouse who is named as executor could also be in a potential conflict of interest situation. For example, where that spouse decides not to accept the provision of her spouse's Will and instead makes a claim against the estate for a share of the family property, she may not be able to act as the executor. In some jurisdictions, the spouse is automatically removed as executor in these circumstances.

Not every potential conflict results in the removal of the named executor. There are situations where an executor is acting in more than one capacity and is entitled to continue to act. For example, the Will may appoint the spouse as the executor *and* the beneficiary of a trust in the Will. As we have seen, as executor, she will have discretion to decide how much she, herself, gets from the estate. Even though in this case, her personal interest and her position as executor conflict with one another she may not be automatically disqualified. The court will take note of the fact that the Will-maker would have been aware of the potential conflict and still decided to name the spouse as both a beneficiary and executor. If the potential conflict was disregarded by the Will-maker, the court may be more willing to accept the conflict.

Similarly, an executor who is also the accountant or the lawyer for the estate can retain both positions. In such case, although there may be a potential conflict, courts will generally wait until an actual conflict of interest arises. These roles are generally compatible and will not necessarily put the personal interests of the executor in actual conflict with those of the estate.

B. Failure to Properly Administer the Estate

A court will not hold an executor to a standard of perfection. Some mistakes made by an executor will not justify his or her removal. Removal only occurs where a court feels that the assets of the estate are in danger.

For example, where an executor has used estate assets for his or her own purposes or acted dishonestly, the court may feel it necessary to remove him or her so that he or she no longer has authority over the estate.

Similarly, where an executor distributes the estate in a manner that is inconsistent with the terms of the Will, the court may find that he or she did not properly appreciate his or her duties and may remove him or her immediately.

Sometimes a Will appoints more than one executor and often there are disagreements among them which cannot easily be resolved. Where the executors cannot agree and the estate is paralyzed, the beneficiaries may suggest that one or more of the executors should be removed. The court may not even be concerned about which of the executors is "at fault." More importantly, the court will consider the best way to get the estate back on course.

In summary, a court will generally remove an executor where it is shown that the estate assets are in danger, the executor acted dishonestly or if it can be proven that the executors are not capable of properly managing the estate.

C. Animosity

Often beneficiaries and executors do not get along. However, generally this alone will not cause the removal of the executor. As mentioned earlier, courts often defer to the Will-maker's choice of executor. The court will generally only remove an executor if the hostility between the executor and beneficiaries is so great that the estate simply cannot be administered in accordance with the terms of the Will.

As we have seen, this scenario arises more often where the executor is empowered to make discretionary decisions, such as the amounts and the timing of payments to the beneficiaries.

If the executor is so hostile to the beneficiaries that it can be shown that he or she cannot impartially and objectively make these decisions, the court may have no choice but to remove him or her.

Before you, as a beneficiary, launch a court application to remove the executor, it may be wise to raise your concerns with the executor in a more informal manner. Sometimes an executor will agree to step down without a battle.

In our experience, applications to remove executors often become very contentious and expensive. What a beneficiary feels is a clear case to remove an executor is not always accepted by a court. The executor has the right to state his or her case as to why he or she should remain in the position. These cases are often seen by the executor as personal attacks on him or her, and on his or her honesty and competence. In most cases, these are strongly defended by the executor to preserve his or her reputation and self-esteem. The executor will likely point out to the court that he or she is trying to preserve the Will-maker's stated wishes appointing him or her as executor.

In many cases, the legal costs of the executor and beneficiaries, even where the beneficiary is successful in removing the executor, will be paid from the estate. In essence, at least some of these legal fees may come out of the beneficiary's pocket.

In addition to being costly, convincing a court to remove an executor is often very difficult. Unless it is clear and obvious that an executor should be removed, beneficiaries should carefully weigh the cost and difficulty of removing an executor. Removal of an executor should be thought of as a last resort.

4.   COURT INTERPRETATION OF A WILL

Wills are drafted with wording designed to be understood by lawyers and judges. By definition, the Will-maker is dead when the Will becomes relevant. Therefore, even if the Will-maker understood what was meant by a certain phrase or word, he or she is not around to explain it. If the lawyers are unsure of the meaning of a Will, a court application to interpret it may be necessary.

When a lawyer properly drafts a Will, he or she expresses the intentions of the Will-maker using language, terms, phrases, and even references to the Latin language, which may not be familiar either to the Will-maker or the beneficiaries. However, this legalese has been used in Wills for hundreds of years and has been interpreted by many courts. Therefore, when lawyers see this legalese, they immediately understand how the Will works. If the lawyers for the beneficiary and the lawyers for the executor both agree on what the words mean, there is no need to ask a court to interpret the Will. However, where a word, term or phrase in a Will can be interpreted in more than one way, trouble can arise.

There are many examples of Wills that likely made perfect sense to the Will-maker, but which cannot be understood by the beneficiaries or their lawyers. Even words like "children" or "nephews" can be the subject of court interpretation:

> Is a step child or an adopted child within the definition of "child"? In some jurisdictions, for example, the legal definition of "child" includes adopted children, but excludes step children.

> When the Will-maker divided his estate equally among his "nephews," did he mean to include his wife's sister's children or only his brother's children?

Another real-life example involved the definition of "relatives":

> The Will-maker had family in both North America and Germany. He made a Will in Germany, leaving all of the estate to be distributed to his "relatives." The German relatives argued that the term "relatives" meant only German relatives, while the North American relatives argued that the term included all of the relatives of the deceased. The trial court agreed with the German relatives. The North American relatives successfully appealed that court judgment, and overturned the conclusions reached by the trial court. However, the cost of fighting both at the trial and appeal levels was so great that the majority of the estate was used up to fund the legal expenses.

Another case involved a bitter dispute over the meaning of "all of my money."

> The beneficiary who was left "all of my money" claimed not only the cash in the bank, but also all of the stocks and bonds and other investments of the deceased. That led to a court fight over whether the phrase "all of my money" was limited to cash in the bank, as opposed to including other assets. Once again, the estate suffered serious legal expenses in determining the correct meaning of this loosely used term. As it turned out, the court determined that "all of my money" was confined to cash in bank accounts. To prove there is no absolute certainty in these cases, other courts have come to an opposite interpretation of the meaning of the term "money."

We often come across "do-it-yourself" Will kits. Many of these homemade or Will-kit Wills often contain imprecise and confusing language, which can create costly conflict among those who inherit.

Here is how things can go wrong:

Since you were a kid, you and your dad collected cameras. Dad had a collection of 10 vintage cameras. Mom had a lot of antique furniture that went to Dad when Mom died. Dad proceeded to make a home-made Will, leaving your sister all of the "antiques," and leaving you the rest of his "personal possessions."

As you and your sister go through his personal effects after Dad passes away, fighting is the last thing you have on your mind. However, your sister takes the camera collection home with her, insisting that these are part of the "antiques" to which she is entitled. You know that Dad could never have intended to give these to her. Frustration and anger builds, and the words "if only" come to your mind: *if only* Dad could have foreseen this, he would never have been so loose in his wording.

You might have the right to the camera collection if the court finds that the word "antiques" does not include the camera collection. The problem is that your own lawyer says that the law is unclear as to how the word "antiques" will be interpreted in your case. The fact is that if you decide to take this to court, you will be fighting over the meaning of *one* word in Dad's Will.

Where the court is called upon to interpret a provision in a Will, the legal fees of all of the parties are often paid out of the estate. Since the problem was caused by the Will-maker's imprecise language, his estate, and not the beneficiaries, pay the legal costs of determining the meaning of the Will.

5. DISPUTES INVOLVING MENTALLY INCAPABLE PERSONS

Only death triggers the Will. Mental incapacity does not. Even the best planned Will has no effect during the lifetime of the Will-maker.

With an aging population and advancements in medical science allowing people to live longer, mental incapacity is becoming more common in our society.

As discussed earlier, disputes regarding mentally incapable people usually fall into two categories: where there is a Power of Attorney in existence or where there is no Power of Attorney.

a) Where there is a Power of Attorney

In most jurisdictions, every adult is allowed to appoint someone else to act on his or her behalf if he or she becomes incapable of managing his or her assets or of making healthcare decisions. The appointment must be made in a formal written document known as a Power of Attorney. Depending on where you live, it may be known as a "Durable," "Continuing" or "Enduring". Power of Attorney. In addition, most jurisdictions allow you to have a separate Power of Attorney dealing with your money and assets and another one dealing with medical decisions or personal care. A Power of Attorney must be made while the person making it still has sufficient mental capacity. However, once the person dies, his or her Power of Attorney is automatically terminated. At this point, his or her Will comes into effect.

As we have mentioned, the person you appoint to look after your financial affairs or to make healthcare decisions for you is called an "Attorney." The word "Attorney," when dealing with a Power of Attorney, does not mean a lawyer. It means the person appointed as representative under a Power of Attorney.

The Attorney for financial affairs is very much like an executor of a Will. He or she is responsible to properly manage the assets and the financial affairs of the incapable person. He or she must make sure that the assets are protected, decide how to invest them and collect all available income and benefits, including investment interest, government benefits and pensions. The attorney must also decide how to spend the incapable person's money. This is where the fights can begin. Here are a couple of real-life examples:

Mom named her eldest child, Jim, as her Attorney in her financial Power of Attorney. Mom became incapable and Jim started to manage her affairs. Her daughter, Debbie, was a 50-50 beneficiary of Mom's estate. When Debbie asked Jim if everything was ok with Mom's affairs, he told her that Mom was running out of money. Debbie knew that before Mom got sick, Mom had a large nest egg from Dad's estate. She wondered, "Where did all of Mom's money go?" The truth came out after lawyers got involved. Jim had invested most of Mom's money in the stock market. Those stocks fell in value and left Mom's estate with only a fraction of its original value. The fight between Debbie and Jim began before Mom even died.

In another case, a daughter was named as her Mom's Attorney. She was living with, and caring for, Mom. Mom was a diabetic, had serious heart disease, was incontinent, had glaucoma and Parkinson's disease, breast cancer had spread to her bones, and she suffered from Alzheimer's. When required to account for Mom's money, the daughter had few receipts and had paid out large sums of Mom's money in cash. In trying to explain where Mom's money had gone, the daughter stated that much of the money was spent on clothing for Mom. This was not believed by the trial judge, especially the purchases at a lingerie store, in light of Mom's grave medical condition. The daughter was required to repay Mom for the money that couldn't be accounted for.

These are examples taken from real life showing the types of fights that can occur. Often, fights of this nature arise after the death of the parent who made the Power of Attorney. It is often only after the parent's death that the beneficiaries discover that the parent's estate is less than they thought it should be. In most jurisdictions, a beneficiary or the executor of the parent's estate may be entitled to review and challenge the actions of the Attorney that occurred during the parent's lifetime.

From our experience, we find that Attorneys are often shocked that their siblings are challenging them on the management of their parent's affairs. It is not surprising to hear an Attorney comment:

"Don't you trust me? Where were you when I was spending hours upon hours helping Mom and preserving her assets for you? How ungrateful!"

The Attorney, like the executor, must keep very detailed records. He or she must expect to be challenged on every decision he or she makes. An Attorney, like an executor, should get legal advice regarding his or her duties and what he or she can and cannot do.

The beneficiaries will be examining whether the Attorney was using the incapable person's money as his own. Was he using her phone lines to make long-distance calls? Taking Mom on trips to exotic locations? Having Mom make gifts to his children?

If you suspect that the Attorney is not properly managing the incapable person's affairs, you can take the following steps:

- Contact the Attorney and indicate your concerns.

- Contact the government agency in your area that oversees vulnerable and incapable people and ask them to investigate.

- Go to court and request an accounting and perhaps the removal of the Attorney.

As discussed earlier, in many jurisdictions, you can also make a separate Power of Attorney outlining your wishes with respect to medical treatment or personal-care decisions. Depending on where you live, these documents may be referred to as a Power of Attorney for Personal Care, a Power of Attorney for Health Care, a Living Will or an Advanced Health Directive.

Like Wills, the validity of a Power of Attorney can be challenged. If the Power of Attorney is found to be invalid, the court may appoint another person to look after the incapable person's affairs. This person appointed by the court may be known as a "Guardian," "Conservator" or "Committee."

Powers of Attorney are most commonly challenged on the basis that the person who gave the Power of Attorney was not mentally capable at the time it was signed. Usually, challenges such as this occur because some other person or relative is concerned about the way the incapable person's money or health care is being managed.

b)   Where there is No Power of Attorney

Not surprisingly, the absence of a valid financial or health-care Power of Attorney often leads to disputes. The most common disputes are:

- Where there is an argument over whether the parent is incapable or not.

     Here is a typical example:

     Dad's memory is getting worse. He is mixing up names and last week he forgot that he had left the stove on. Unlike ever before, Dad is overly generous with his money, giving away large birthday gifts to friends and relatives. You are very concerned about Dad and believe that he no longer can manage his own affairs. Your brother disagrees. He chalks up Dad's behaviour as normal for a man his age. You think Dad might hurt himself, so you want him to be assessed and have someone appointed to look after his affairs. Your brother thinks you are just trying to get access to Dad's money. Your brother tells you that he will fight on Dad's behalf to keep Dad's independence. You believe that your brother is going to persuade Dad to resist anyone assessing his mental capacity.

- Where it is accepted by everyone that the parent is mentally incapable, but there is a dispute as to who will apply to look after the parent's assets and personal care.

    Here is how a dispute might unfold:

    Although you and your older brother never see eye to eye on anything, the one thing you agree on is that Dad has severe Alzheimer's and can no longer manage his financial affairs. You live in the same city as Dad, but your brother lives out of town, about 2 hours away. Your brother has a successful business and because of this, thinks he should be the one to look after Dad's finances. You believe that he is not a completely honest and up-front person. You spend much more time with Dad and have informally been helping him with paying his bills. You know, deep in your heart, that Dad would want you to look after his affairs, not your brother. For these reasons, you want to be appointed as Dad's guardian. Your brother tells you that under no circumstances will he agree to you being Dad's guardian. Similarly, you tell your brother that Dad would never have wanted him to be in control. Next step—court.

- Where there is a dispute regarding personal care or medical decisions.

    We don't have to look farther than the news to see examples of these types of disputes:

    The *Schiavo* case pitted Terry Schiavo's parents against Terry's spouse. The issue was over whether she should be kept alive or allowed to die after suffering a serious accident. This case went to the highest court. Sadly, there are many similar cases that never make it into the news, but are just as devastating to the families.

    Even more common are disputes regarding whether an aging parent is better off in his or her own home, or in a nursing home. The children will have their own views on what they believe is best for their parent. A child may say that he knows that Dad never wanted to be in a nursing home under any circumstances. Another child might have an expert report showing that it is in Dad's best interest to be in a nursing home. The other children may be stuck in the middle or forced to side with one sibling or another. The family is being ripped apart and it has nothing to do with money.

Capacity litigation is unlike any other type of estate litigation. The parent who is the subject of the litigation is still alive, but likely not aware of the Family War being waged by his or her children over what they feel is best.

Some clients refuse to proceed with litigation while their parent is alive. If they do litigate, they will have to name their parent as a party to the lawsuit, in effect suing their parent. To some, this is demeaning and disrespectful to the parent and they would rather do nothing than involve their parent in this kind of family battle.

CHAPTER 5

CAUSES OF ESTATE LITIGATION: IT'S NOT THE MONEY, IT'S THE PRINCIPLE.

1. IS YOUR FAMILY AT RISK?

As you think of a family torn by conflict, your first emotion might be one of hope that your family will not be caught. While we acknowledge that family conflicts exist, we may not expect them to occur in our family.

As Wills lawyers, we understand how the death or incapacity of a loved one can have a dramatic emotional effect on the family. A death might be so unexpected as to shock those who were close to the deceased. In other circumstances, family members may have witnessed many years of a loved one's physical or mental deterioration where death may represent a merciful ending to suffering.

Against this background, it is not surprising that emotions will surface. Sometimes those emotions are immediate, and sharp conflict will erupt over funeral preparations, the contents of a death notice, manner of burial, contents and delivery of the eulogy, and even the choice of casket. Other times, those emotions brew and fester within. The weight of the passing of a parent who was always there for his children may be surreal; it may at first have a numbing effect. Perhaps the emotions are subdued throughout the mourning process, but then later surface, and when they do, it is not uncommon for the bereaved to feel anger. Such anger may find its direction in the form of hostility towards the attending physician or the hospital staff. Other times, anger has been brewing for years. In our experience, it is not uncommon to come across children who have felt ignored, unappreciated and have buried such feelings during the life of the parent. Now with the passing of that parent, the feelings emerge in the form of anger. That anger may easily be directed at siblings who, in the mind of the angry child, received preferential treatment by the parent. The parent is no longer there to answer for these feelings.

The passing of a significant loved one will likely unleash a potent mixture of love, hate, guilt, anger, jealousy and a host of other emotions. It might be said that, in essence, the Family War is the use of the legal system to address one or more of these emotions.

The following circumstances can all contribute to the outbreak of a Family War. Some are much more likely to cause conflict than others. Examination of these key circumstances may help predict the likelihood that your family will be involved in an estate fight. This examination is not scientific and the contribution of any one factor to an estate dispute differs from case to case:

2. HOW LIKELY IS AN ESTATE FIGHT?

a) The Deceased Died without a Will

Based upon the observations and legal experience of the authors, when the deceased dies without a Will, there is an increased risk of family conflict.

In most jurisdictions, the law sets out a list of heirs who are entitled to inherit when there is no Will. The law recognizes blood lines and marriage, but ignores factors such as friendship and gratitude. Friends or relatives who cared for, or were financially supported by, the deceased during his or her lifetime will not be specially recognized in the distribution of the estate. This may lead to claims for unpaid services provided to the deceased or dependant support claims.

Furthermore, the fact that there is no Will means that there is no executor appointed. In order for someone to have authority to move the frozen estate forward, that someone must be appointed with the consent of those entitled to inherit by law. No one can assume that there will be agreement with respect to such appointment. In our experience, we have seen a great number of disputes among surviving children, which arise over the naming of one or more representatives to administer the estate of a person who died without a Will. One son may insist that he is the appropriate one to deal with the estate, and that his sister is not as capable or as trustworthy as he is. The sister, insulted and offended, may challenge her brother, and a fight is likely to result.

b)   The Deceased Died with a Homemade Will.

As we have previously discussed, Wills are documents that require precision in expressing the intentions of those who won't be there to explain them. For this and other reasons, those who attempt to express themselves through a will-kit or a home-made Will run a risk that there will be misunderstanding and misinterpretation after they pass away. It is no wonder that some will-kits have disclaimer language to protect those who publish them.

Also, a homemade Will exposes the estate to risks. Even if the language is proper, it may be challenged on the basis that it does not comply with the legal requirements for a valid Will, such as proper witnessing.

As more and more people attempt to write their own Wills without professional assistance, we expect this to be a more common cause of estate litigation.

"Why would Dad have done this to our family?" Those tearful words of one of our clients still echo in our ears. Dad could not invest the time or the money to make a proper Will to deal with his estate. Dad's badly prepared will-kit tore apart the fabric of his family.

c) The Estate Has No Valuable Assets

"Can't split a painting on the wall or share a table in the hall."

These words are from the song entitled *The Family Fight*, co-written by Les Kotzer, one of the authors of this book.

Many Family Wars are fights over items with great sentimental value, but little monetary value. How can you put a price on Mom's wedding ring that was on her finger for decades? To her children, the ring may be worth fighting for.

Bearing in mind human nature, it is not surprising to see how easily conflict among siblings is created. So many people are lulled into a false sense of security, feeling that without valuable assets, no one will fight. However in our experience, battles among children are very often over memories rather than money.

Unless it is well planned out, the distribution of personal effects carries a high risk of creating bad feelings, which can cause a Family War.

d) A Deathbed Will is Signed.

Contrast two scenarios:

Imagine Dad, a healthy 61 year old businessman, having arranging a meeting with his lawyer and accountant for early next month to discuss making his Will. He prepares for that meeting by looking through his investments and his other assets. He finds some quiet time to recall the gifts he gave to each of his three children up to that point in time. He summarizes, for himself, the financial positions of each of his children. He also develops some questions regarding the uncertainties he has as to what their expectations are. Basically he is concerned with equality, but also realizes that there must be some deviations from equality and notes that there are some delicate discussions he must have with the children on this point, even before his meeting. There are other considerations that enter into this situation, particularly after he has met with the accountant and the lawyer, and after he has heard from each of the children with respect to the delicate matters. Such delicate matters might include, among other things, the distribution among his children of his personal items and other family heirlooms, and the disposition of the shares in his company, from which only one of his children is making a living.

Now imagine Dad, now an ill 85 year old, having omitted all of the discussions, considerations and planning described in the above paragraph. He is lying in a hospital bed suffering from a terminal illness. His immediate world is a hospital room. In this context, Dad will now pull together his last-minute thoughts in the form of a Will that he makes himself. He struggles with the immediacy of this situation, so urgent that there is no quiet time, no time to consult with professionals or with his children. He takes what to him is the path of least resistance. He leaves everything equally to the three children. He names the eldest child as the executor.

Picture how the other children feel when they find out that Dad's Will did not "even out" the numerous gifts given by Dad during his lifetime to one of the children. Imagine the insult that the younger children might feel at being overlooked as executors, despite their talents, education and close relationship with Dad. It is in this context that the seeds are sown for the temptation to challenge this last-minute Will. Did Dad really have capacity? Was he subject to undue influence from the executor-brother, especially because he had been a frequent visitor, alone, just himself and Dad?

In a word, procrastinating Dad managed to take the "planning" out of "estate planning." Because of his deathbed Will, he left a legacy of turmoil for his family.

e) Mom or Dad Becomes Mentally Incapable

When we speak of procrastination in estate planning, our concerns do not end with the preparation of a valid Will. It is frightening to think of how many parents have failed to prepare valid Powers of

Attorney. They take false comfort because they feel that a Will is all they need. The disturbing aspect is their failure to address what will happen in their families if they become mentally incapacitated before they die. They have not provided for someone they trust to step in and manage their finances and assets or their medical and personal care decisions.

The dispute becomes a struggle for power and control and may be fought in front of a judge or government regulator, depending on where you live. To gain control, each child may try to show how and why he or she is preferable to his or her sibling as the person to administer Mom's affairs. The process might create hostility between siblings, as each attempts to show why his or her rival sibling is not appropriate to be granted the authority.

f)   Children are Treated Differently in the Will.

In order to appreciate what motivates a child to retain a lawyer to fight his or her siblings, imagine this: step into the shoes of a child who discovers, by reading Mom's Will, that he has received a smaller portion of her estate than any of his other siblings. It is easy to feel his hurt, as if Mom loved the others more than she loved him. There are occasions where Mom, if well advised prior to her death, might have left an explanatory letter along with her Will, indicating the reasons she chose to lessen the share of a particular child. Such a letter may have gone a very long way toward soothing or even eliminating his sense of hurt and his motivation to sue. However, in the absence of such an explanatory letter, the hurt that a child feels can easily drive him towards breaking his relationship with his siblings, and attacking the Will.

These feelings can arise so easily from a child's failure of memory or a parent's failure to communicate.

For example, what might have been apparent to Mom was that this child was the only one of her three children who got all of his college tuition and residency fees paid.

The son chooses not to remember this special treatment from his Mom.

To Mom, this child benefited more than any of his other siblings—the others did not go to college. Looking at the situation from Mom's point of view, she had every reason to reduce the entitlement of this one child under her Will. These considerations motivated Mom to increase the share to her other two children in order to equalize what she gave to her son.

The sad part is that Mom failed to share her reasoning with the son, who now wants to challenge her Will.

Many children view their parent's Will as a last expression of love. Therefore, if a child is treated differently from his sibling in the Will, he may feel the need to challenge the Will in order to protect his own feelings of worthiness.

Aside from emotional pressure, a child's spouse may encourage him to contest Mom's Will. For example, spouses can sometimes add fuel to the fire with comments like:

"Aren't you as good as your brother and sister?" or

"You shouldn't accept less. They were your parents too."

g)   There are Children from Different Relationships

In today's world, parents often marry more than once. Children may be born from a first or subsequent marriage or from a common law relationship. A step-mother may not have the same attachment to her step-children as she does to her own children. Also, the children may not have the same attachment to their "half"-siblings as they do to their "full"-siblings.

Let us look at Dad, who, after his first wife passed away, started a relationship with another person.

Dad has two children from his first marriage, both of whom finished college. After he lost his first wife, Dad remarried and with his new wife had another child, who is now ten years old. On the surface, it would appear that there are no difficulties here. Delving deeper, however, the trigger for potential conflict becomes apparent.

When Dad passes away, the family relationship may be affected by various factors, some of which can be summarized as follows:

Shared memories of childhood

The two children from Dad's first marriage have shared childhood memories, such as trips, picnics, movies, parties and common friendships. In essence, they shared childhood together. None of these experiences have been shared between them and their half-sibling from Dad's second marriage.

Dad's Will leaves a much greater gift to the child of his second marriage than it does to either of the children from his first marriage.

Dad's reasoning for this plan makes sense. He had paid for the two older children's college education. Dad knew that, given the sharp rise in college tuition fees, his youngest child would need considerably more help from him. He ensured that his young child would get that help by structuring his Will so that more money was left to that child.

When Dad dies, the older children feel hurt that Dad preferred the young child over them in his Will. As logical as Dad's thinking was, we find, in our experience, that without the moderating element of shared memories, there may be nothing to soften the feelings of hurt and jealousy. These types of feelings fester. Jealousy and bitterness are not good ingredients for fostering family harmony.

Influence of the step parent

Suppose that the above example were altered so that Dad left more to his older children than to the child of his second marriage. The second wife may be very upset at the way her child is being treated under her husband's Will. The second wife will most likely have a stronger bond with her own child than with her husband's children from his first marriage. Because she may not have a bond with her step-children, there may be little, other than the cost factor, to discourage her from launching an attack on the Will, or claiming some form of dependant's support on behalf of her own child.

h)   The Parent Remarries.

Even where the second spouse does not have her own children, conflicts often arise between the "second" spouse and children from a prior relationship.

Dad may want to make provision for his second wife as well as for his children from his first marriage. A clear conflict is built into this situation. In order to keep everyone satisfied, Dad must perform a careful balancing act. Often, however, either one or both groups are disappointed with whatever Dad decides to do.

Dad has a number of options, each carrying its own problems.

He may choose to leave his entire estate to his second wife in the hope that she will respect his wishes and leave anything left over when she dies to his children. This almost always causes concern for the children, since there is very little legal protection for them. In most jurisdictions, she is not required to fulfill Dad's wish and may spend all the money on herself or leave it to someone else, including a future spouse.

Another option is for Dad to put his estate in trust for the lifetime of his second wife. In this situation, the children will have to wait until the second wife dies before getting anything. From the second wife's point of view, she may feel that the children are just "waiting for her to die" to get their money. In addition, they will be watching over how the money is spent. The second wife may end up having to explain to her step-children why she a needs a vacation or a new car. This option continues to link the two groups in a situation that has inherent conflict.

Lastly, Dad could decide to divide the estate between his second wife and the children. Among other tax and financial concerns, the provision may end up being inadequate for either the second wife or the children, causing one or both to seek further support from the estate.

Perhaps more than any other family circumstance, a subsequent marriage or relationship leads to bad feelings and conflict. That conflict can occur among the children themselves and between some or all of the children and the second spouse or partner.

i)   One of the Siblings is Estranged from the Family.

Where a child is estranged or perceived to be estranged from the family, many problems can result. Regardless of how the situation is treated, conflict can arise:

(a)   After a major blow-up with his Dad, the child completely cuts himself off from the family. No one even has his address or telephone number. If Dad decides to include the estranged child as an equal beneficiary in his Will, the other children who were close to Dad may be upset. They may feel that their obligation to share the estate equally with the estranged child is unfair. Bitterness and conflict may result.

(b)   The child did not maintain much contact with Mom, not because of bitterness, but because of his busy life and his own family obligations. His siblings form the impression that he is estranged from Mom. However this child feels that he is as much of a child to Mom as his siblings are. Although he calls Mom on her birthday and on Mother's Day, the other children don't believe he cares about her. On the other hand, he feels entitled to participate equally with them in dividing Mom's estate. Mom's Will provides less for him than for his siblings. The battle lines are drawn between a son, who believes it is his birthright to be treated equally with his siblings, and his siblings, who feel, based on their own perception of his relationship with Mom, that he is not entitled to be treated equally.

Finding that he is deprived leads to his impression that his siblings may have exercised undue influence on Mom. He may believe that the other children contributed to whatever estrangement existed between him and Mom. For example, he may think that his brothers and sisters were badmouthing him to Mom or excluding him from family functions.

However, from the point of view of the siblings, they feel that aside from infrequent contact from this child on birthdays and holidays, he essentially led his own life away from the family. They may also feel that the estranged child had no real feelings for Mom and is only surfacing now in order to assert his claim to her estate.

As we have seen, conflicts can easily arise, regardless of whether the estranged child is included or excluded from the Will. Either way, someone is bound to be upset.

j)   Children Living in Different Locations

In many cases, the burden of administering an estate or assisting an incapable parent with his or her finances or personal care is not shared equally among all of the children. If one child lives in the same city as a parent, geography may impose a burden on this child that his or her siblings escape simply because of the fact that they live out of town.

Problems occur when that child's efforts are not properly recognized. An example would be a claim for compensation against the estate for services rendered by that child to the parent. The other siblings might be inclined to oppose that claim on the grounds that the services provided should have been out of love for the parent and not for financial gain. Acrimony is likely to result if these other siblings feel that the claim by the claimant-child is only a "money grab" and that the parent did not intend to compensate that child.

Though not as contentious as some of the other circumstances that we have discussed, this common family situation has the potential to create a rift in the family.

k)   Children with Different Levels of Financial Resources

Imagine a situation where a widower makes a Will that attempts to address a financial imbalance between two of his children. To the best of Dad's knowledge and understanding, his son Peter is very wealthy, and his other son, Robert is not. He loves both sons very much. However, in his Will, Dad gives Robert a substantially greater share of his estate than Peter for the simple reason that he feels Robert needs the financial help.

In some circumstances, this will cause bad feelings and potentially litigation.

For example, suppose Dad's impression of Peter's wealth is incorrect. Peter may drive an expensive car, live in a big house and have a high lifestyle, but be in debt. The car may be leased, the house may have a big mortgage and his high lifestyle may be financed by credit. When Dad dies, the reason for the disproportionate treatment comes out. Peter will, no doubt, be upset and may consider challenging Dad's Will based on the fact that Dad didn't know what he was doing.

Alternatively, imagine that Peter really was wealthy. He may justifiably feel that he has earned that wealth through his hard work. He may also feel that Robert's financial difficulties are his own fault due to laziness or bad judgment. The result is that Peter believes that he is being punished for being successful. This belief may undermine the relationship between Peter and Robert.

Like all situations where children are treated unequally, a Will that distributes the estate based on the relative financial resources of the beneficiaries can spark a family battle.

l) The Will deals with the Family Home, the Cottage or a Family Business.

Sometimes, the type of assets dealt with in an estate increases the risk of a Family War. Let us examine three special assets, which can lead to conflict.

A.   The Family Home

After parents die, the family home can be an explosive and divisive asset. Fights over the home can occur in many circumstances. Let's look at an example where one child lives at home with the parents and the others do not.

While the parents are alive, the real issues lie dormant. Once the parents are gone, the trouble may begin.

Here is a dramatic illustration:

Imagine that your divorced sister lives with Mom in Mom's home. She has no money to move out. In order to allow her to have a roof over her head, Mom's Will makes a special provision that will allow her to live in the home for the rest of her life or until she no longer wants to live there.   Only when that occurs will you receive any share of the family home. Furthermore, Mom's Will provides that the expenses for maintaining the home, while your sister is living there, will be paid from Mom's estate. This will further reduce what you will receive from Mom's estate.

When Mom dies, you may be upset because you think Mom unfairly benefited your sister. You will have no access to the equity in that home until your sister passes away. You may receive nothing since there is no guarantee that you will survive your sister. You may be concerned over the way your sister maintains the family home. If she doesn't maintain it properly, the family home will deteriorate in value. As a result, your share will be reduced. On the other hand, if she does maintain the home, the cost of maintenance and repairs comes out of the estate, which also reduces your share.

Did Mom really mean to do that?

Thoughts of asking your sister to leave and sell the home may cross your mind. But to your sister, Mom's home is *her* home. She cannot bear the thought of selling it and moving to an apartment.

On the other hand, let's assume Mom did not make a special provision in her Will for the family home. Instead, she leaves her entire estate equally between you and your sister. This means that you will have an equal entitlement to the home with your sister. Your sister might fear that your intention is to sell the home and force her out. You are caught in the middle between realizing your fair share and fulfilling your sister's desires. If you agree that she can live in the family home, you may have to insist that she buy your half out. If she has no money, how can both of you be accommodated?

This is just the tip of the iceberg when the family home is involved in an estate.

B.   The Family Cottage

We will never forget how one client told us that it was the treasured family cottage that tore his family apart. Just like the family home, there are many different situations involving the family cottage that can lead to an estate battle.

Imagine a family with three grown children, each with their own families. They all have deep attachments to the cottage. These attachments have formed early in their lives because of the vivid, happy memories of weekends and vacations. Can a cottage be divided three ways?

Suppose the parents try:

Who gets the cottage on the long weekends, the national holidays and the prime weeks of summer?

What if one of the kids is a 'neat freak' and the others are less than tidy?

How are the expenses going to be shared?

Will all of the children use the cottage for exactly the same amount of time? If they don't, will they be able to work out a method for dividing the expenses fairly?

What if one of the children cannot afford his or her share?

Who looks after the emergencies if there is a flood or the snow buckles the roof or a fire causes damage?

All of these issues can cause friction and, potentially, a battle among family members.

The alternatives are not much better.

Sometimes parents will give a child the right to buy the cottage from the estate. However, giving one child this option to purchase the cottage is not a perfect solution either. If the parents do not wish to prefer one child over the other in giving the option, the Will may state that the selection is made randomly. In some cases, the children flip a coin or pick a number out of a hat. However, regardless of who is selected, the other children lose their connection with the family cottage. That often leads to hurt feelings and strained relationships.

Some parents may try and avoid these problems by selling the cottage, either before death or requiring a sale immediately after their death. In either case, this means that there is no continuing legacy of the family cottage. However, at least there is no cottage to fight over.

As we have seen, there is no perfect solution to the potential problems created by a family cottage. Even the best planning may not always avoid a Family War over the cottage.

C.   The Family Business

The family business is another potentially divisive asset. This is clearly an asset that requires very delicate treatment to avoid conflict among family members left to inherit from the owner who passes away.

Imagine that Dad has three sons. The eldest son worked with Dad for many years in the family business. His two younger brothers did not. The eldest son who worked with Dad expected to inherit the business, since he devoted many years to building it up. The business has always had his full time and attention.

Dad has several choices:

Let's say he leaves his estate, including the business, equally to all three children. This means that all of the children will have an equal share in the business. Could this create bad feelings that could lead to a dispute?

- The working son may feel that all of his hard work in building the business over the past many years has not been recognized in Dad's Will.

- The working son might not work as hard as he has in the past, since his non-working siblings will be benefiting from the fruits of his hard work.

- What if the younger sons want to become involved in the business? Will they all be able to get along in the business?

- What happens when one of the siblings dies? Will the deceased's brother's spouse be a partner in the business?

- Will the non-working children agree with what the working son feels he should be paid for running the business?

- What if the business goes under? Who will be blamed?

- If the working son considers buying out his siblings, how will the business be valued?

Dad has another choice.

He might leave the business to the working son and give his other children assets that he feels are equal to the value of the business.

This option can create just as many problems as the first option. For one thing, it would be very difficult for Dad to predict what the exact value of the business will be at the time of his death. Between the time of making the Will and the time of his death, the fortunes of the business could rise or fall, even to the point of insolvency, leaving the inheriting son with either a windfall or a valueless asset. At the same time, the assets given to the other children, such as an investment property or a cottage, might have risen or declined in value. It would be highly unusual for the assets to remain of equivalent value over a period of years, or even months.

Another option is for Dad's Will to require the executor to obtain an independent valuation of the business at the time of Dad's death. The business will go to the working son, with the equivalent value in assets going to the other sons. However, the estate may not have sufficient other assets to make the equivalent gifts to the other sons. In that case, perhaps his Will requires the working son to "purchase" the business from the estate. Assuming that there are sufficient other assets in the estate or that the working son can afford to purchase the business, this option may ensure that the children each receive an equivalent amount.

However, a legacy of resentment may still be the result.

The children who did not get the business may watch the business thrive after their father's death. They may feel that they should be part of its success because it was Dad's business

While Dad was alive and running his grocery store, he was always generous with his children. They all developed the routine of filling their household needs from the stock in the store. What happens when the business is transferred to one son? The working son may deny his siblings the privilege of taking stock out of the store. How will those siblings feel about the change?

The resentment may never go away.

Here are a few other issues involving the family business that can cause arguments:

Imagine that of three sons, two worked with Dad. During his life, Dad may have had to arbitrate issues between the two working sons. Once Dad is no longer in a position to arbitrate, how are the conflicts avoided?

Dad was partner with his brother in the business and always protected his working son from his partner. When Dad passes away, the son who inherits the business may quickly be drawn into serious conflict with Dad's surviving partner, who takes on the role of a dominant and overbearing uncle.

As we have seen, the family business is a difficult asset to deal with after a death. Regardless of what choices are made, potentially bad feelings and resentment can result. This, in turn, can tear a once-close family apart.

3.   SOME GOOD NEWS

We have looked at a number of circumstances that may increase the chance of an estate fight. Now we will look at one circumstance that may actually reduce the likelihood of a Family War.

As we have seen, when children are surprised at the contents of their parent's Will, they often believe that the Will does not reflect their parent's true wishes. Carried to the extreme, such a belief may turn into a Will challenge, based on claims that Mom was pressured or that she did not really understand what she was saying in her Will.

From our experience it seems that conflicts between children can often be avoided by parent-child communication. The jealousies, bad feelings and misunderstandings that might otherwise arise can be minimized when parents explain their intentions and reasoning to their children.

There is no set formula for communicating intentions to beneficiaries. We have seen clients who meet with their children one on one or as a group. Others wishing to avoid direct confrontation have used a letter or even an explanatory video setting out their reasoning and choices. A relatively new phenomenon is the use of a neutral facilitator to assist parents in discussing these potentially divisive issues with their family. Often these facilitators are experienced estate lawyers or mediators.

Hearing explanations from the parents themselves in their own voice or words may reduce the risk of a Will challenge.

4. MOTIVATION FOR ESTATE LITIGATION

You may be wondering how your brother could be so adamant in the claim he is making against the estate, or why your sister is defending her position so strongly. Understanding the motivation of your brother or sister will be valuable in developing your strategy and increasing the chances of settlement.

Estate litigation is not always about legal positions. Emotions can cause conflict whether there is a legal basis or not. All it takes is the court filing fee to start a lawsuit.

It is extremely rare for a litigant to justify estate litigation on the basis of greed. Most will insist and truly believe that "It's not about money…it's about *principle*." Since it cannot be seen as a fight over Mom's money, the parties will usually justify and rationalize their respective positions as an expression of principle, not greed.

Despite its many forms, almost all estate litigation is rationalized by the parties in one of, or a combination of, two ways:

> a) It's (or It's not) what Mom *really* wanted!; and

> b) It's not fair!

These are not grounds for challenging a Will. However, they are often the emotional drivers that underlie the legal challenges.

a) "It's (not) what Mom REALLY wanted!"

When a child believes that the estate of his or her parent is not being distributed the way Mom or Dad intended, that child may feel justified in challenging the Will of that parent.

For example, Mom's Will may be challenged if the child believes that Mom did not have mental capacity at the time that she made her Will. The challenging child may feel justified in litigating because he or she does not believe that the Will reflects Mom's true intentions. The child believes that if Mom really knew what she was doing, and was "with it," she never would have prepared that particular Will.

The child might challenge the Will on other grounds, such as having a feeling that Mom was pressured by another sibling when she made her Will. His or her thinking might be, "If Mom had not been influenced by my brother, she would never have done her Will this way."

Often, in the case of older Wills, another type of justification surfaces. Mom's 25-year-old Will may have left everything equally to all of her children. The challenging child remembers that 5 years ago Mom promised him a larger share of the estate, or a special gift. Her old Will fails to reflect her subsequent promise to him. When he raises this complaint to his siblings, they insist that everyone has to abide by "Mom's last Will." His only choice is to challenge this "Will" because in his mind it does not truly reflect Mom's *last* wishes.

Another example occurs where Dad's Will left everything to Mom, who now remarries. Mom and her new husband each make a new Will, leaving everything to each other. Mom passes away before her new husband. He inherits everything she owns, which includes everything that her first husband owned and inherited from his relatives. Meanwhile, Mom's children firmly believe that Dad never intended for his money to end up in the hands of strangers, cutting out his own children. When Mom's children raise this issue with her second husband and meet resistance, they challenge her Will because they feel she never *intended* this result.

The decision of the challenging child to launch court proceedings is likely to be met with resistance from the child who is defending the Will. Those defending the Will often believe in their own minds that the Will *does* properly express Mom's true intentions. Just as there are arguments justifying the challenge to the Will, there are also arguments that can be used to justify its validity:

- Mom left me a bigger share because Mom knew I needed the money more than my brothers and sisters did;

- She knew they did not need as much because they were already inheriting money from their in-laws;

- I helped Mom more than any of them did; and

- They didn't help Mom enough.

In effect, both sides will be relying on their view of what Mom *really* wanted to justify their position.

Surprisingly, both sides may be absolutely correct in what Mom told them about her intentions. In our experience, parents often tell one child one story, and another child a different story. For example, a parent may complain to her son about her daughter. The son is left with the impression that the daughter hardly ever came to visit Mom and that Mom was very disappointed in her. Mom, not wanting to upset her daughter, never tells her that she is disappointed. Instead she warmly welcomes her every time she visits and tells her not to worry about coming to see her because she knows how busy she is with her own life. Mom's Will may be viewed by each of the children in the context of what Mom told them. Both children may feel justified in attacking or defending a Will that does not reflect the feelings Mom expressed to them.

In this situation, both sides truly believe that they know what Mom really wanted. The sad fact is that Mom is not around to explain her true feelings. To a degree, Mom is to blame for the litigation, as she told each child a different story and set them up to fight.

Unfortunately, only one side can win. No one, including the judge, will ever know what Mom *really* wanted.

As lawyers sometimes say: Judges decide cases on the *proof*, not necessarily on the *truth*.

b)   "It's Not Fair"

From our experience, estate litigation is often justified in terms of fairness. "I just want what's fair!" is a common expression of motivation or justification in an estate dispute. Of course, what is seen as fair to one person may seem unfair to another.

Let's examine two circumstances where fairness is used to justify involvement in an estate dispute:

> *"I was never treated fairly and I'm still not being treated fairly."*

A Will is often seen as a parent's last expression of love, faith, trust and respect. Children read a lot into what a Will says. They look to see if their beliefs about their relationship with their parents and their siblings are reinforced in black and white. Here are a few examples:

140

- Bill was always the one who took charge of Mom's financial affairs and appeared to the other children to be Mom's preferred child. When Mom dies, the siblings look to see whether this parental bias is reinforced in Mom's Will. Bill receives a larger share of her estate and is appointed as her sole executor. They are very upset that Mom continued the pattern of "unfairness" in her Will. This may motivate them to look to legal grounds to overturn the unfairness.

- John believed that Dad was always bailing out his lazy brother, Dennis, because he could never keep a steady job. This always bothered John because he worked hard and never asked for one penny from Dad. John is upset because he doesn't think it is fair that Dad's Will gives him and his lazy brother the same amount, even though his brother got so much during Dad's lifetime. Will this be enough to push John to finally say "enough is enough!"?

- Mary always felt that Mom did not trust or respect her judgment and decisions. Mary will be eager to see if this lack of trust was reflected in Mom's Will. It turns out that Mary's share of Mom's estate was given to her in trust with strings attached. What does Mary do now?

In each of these examples, one or more of the children may see the parent's Will as a continuation of perceived unfairness that existed during the parent's lifetime. This may be the opportunity to turn their long-held ill feelings into legal action.

For example, in Mary's case, from the time she was very young, she always believed that Mom disapproved of any decision she made. Mom didn't like the boys she dated, she didn't approve of the college that Mary attended, and Mom disliked the man she ended up marrying. On the other hand, in Mary's mind, Mom loved everything that her brother did. He could do no wrong. The fact that Mom treated Mary and her brother so differently caused a great deal of hurt to Mary throughout her life. While Mom was alive, Mary did not want to discuss her feelings with her. Though she felt that she was treated unfairly, she did not want to risk destroying her relationship with her mother.

When Mom dies, in Mary's mind, the unfairness continues. While both Mary and her brother receive the same amount under Mom's Will, they are still treated differently. The brother gets his half immediately and can spend it any way he wants. Mary's half has strings attached. It is tied up in trust for the rest her life. She will only get monthly payments from the executor. She will never be trusted with a lump sum amount from the estate.

What will Mary do about this?

Although she didn't want to confront the unfairness during Mom's lifetime, the gloves may come off now that Mom has died. Some new factors come into play:

- With Mom gone there is no longer a child-parent relationship to maintain. Mary doesn't have to worry about hurting her mother, so she can direct all of her anger towards her brother.

- During Mom's lifetime, Mary had no legal forum to challenge Mom's emotional bias against her and Mom's preference for the brother. While Mom is alive, no court cares about Mary's argument that she is disappointed by the way her mother feels about her. Mary may have expected the unfairness to end with Mom's death. That is not the case. To Mary, Mom's Will only continues the unfairness. The fact that the unfairness was reflected in Mom's Will opens the door for Mary. Mary now has the opportunity to address her lifelong grievances through the legal system by launching an attack on Mom's Will.

- Estate litigation is often a person's last chance to right the perceived wrongs of the past. Mary may never get another chance to stand up for herself and attain fairness at last.

These factors combine to turn a situation that was under control while Mom was alive into a Family War when Mom dies.

"I am not being treated fairly. This has to be a mistake!"

Those who believe that they will be beneficiaries often have expectations of what they *should* get in the Will. The deceased's companion of many years may expect to receive what a married spouse should get. A child who was very close to Dad may expect that his or her relationship will translate into a bigger share of Dad's estate.

When those expectations are dashed, the disappointed beneficiary may be motivated to "do something" about the way the estate is being dealt with.

When Dad died, his estate went to Mom. Of course, all of the children were fine with that. But when Mom dies, she leaves her estate, which really came from Dad, to her new common law spouse. The children may recognize Mom's attachment to her common law spouse and even like him. However the overriding feeling is that it's not fair that their parents' estate is ending up in the hands of strangers. It's completely unfair that the family's estate doesn't stay "in the family."

Take the opposite example. When Mom died, all of her assets went to her children, completely cutting out her common law spouse. The common law spouse feels that he is being treated unfairly. After all, he was the one who made her happy in her final years and who cared for her when she was dying. Her children didn't even mention him at the funeral or in the obituary. He feels that it's not fair that he is being pushed aside with no recognition of the special relationship he had with their mother. Will it be hard for the common law spouse to justify why he commenced a dependant support claim against the estate?

Another example:

The caregiver-child who took Mom shopping and drove her to her doctor's appointments for the last 15 years of her life formed a close bond with her. The caregiver-child was the only one of Mom's three children who really cared for her this way. The caregiver-child perceived her two siblings as indifferent. The caregiver-child may feel that it is unfair to be treated the same way as her siblings, who were distant from Mom for so many years. If Mom's Will does not give more to the caregiver-child, how will she react? Will she try to rectify the perceived unfairness with a claim against Mom's estate for compensation?

In each of these examples, the beneficiary's expectations were not fulfilled. Their expectations were based on what they believed was "fair." Therefore, to them, their treatment under the Will is an unfair mistake.

As we have seen, feelings of unfairness may arise when the Will is read for the first time, or these feelings of unfairness may have evolved over many decades. Regardless, if a person feels strongly that the Will is unfair to him or her, that feeling may, at the very least, motivate him or her to seek legal advice. If his or her feelings are strong enough, he or she may resort to legal proceedings.

One final note on the issue of fairness as it relates to estate litigation: The concept of what is "fair" will differ from person to person. Judges are people too and therefore the concept of fairness is often a factor in a judge's decision. Though judges like to be fair, they have to rely on accepted legal grounds and admissible evidence to justify any decision. To be successful in court, you can bring up "fairness," but that alone will not guarantee success. You will have to go to court with more than just "It's not fair."

5. PERSONALITIES IN ESTATE LITIGATION

Even though every family is different, we often see similarities in the roles and personalities adopted by the participants in an estate fight.

One observation is that people often assume the same roles in an estate dispute that they have played in the family since childhood.

For example, where the eldest child was always the one who bossed around the other siblings, that child will often take on that same role in estate litigation. He or she may resent any challenge to his or her authority and may expect to be the one in control of the estate as the executor. If the parent did not put him or her in control, he or she may seek to exercise that control in some other manner, such as challenging the authority of the other executor, or attempting to oversee every decision made.

Similarly, in estate disputes, it is not unusual for adult children to view their siblings in the same way as they did when they were young children. One client told us that her brother was always "the bully" growing up. When they were young he would order her around to do things for him. If she didn't do what he told her to do, he would make false allegations to their mom and the mother would punish her and not him. Throughout the litigation, this was continually raised by the daughter. "Here he is, doing it again," she would say.

In other types of litigation, you may not know the person you are suing. This is not the case in estate litigation. In most estate disputes involving families, the participants know each other better than anyone else in the world. Knowing who you are up against is an extremely important factor in deciding your strategy.

Against this background, we will examine some of the more common roles that seem to emerge over and over again in our estate practice.

a)   The Controller

The personality of The Controller tends to reflect a history of "getting his own way." The Controller is used to having a position of authority, and expects that others will yield to his or her views. There is only harmony when he or she gets his or her own way. He or she will do anything he or she can to impose his or her own views on anyone who might stand in the way.

Here are examples of how The Controller's personality can play out in an estate dispute.

Imagine that The Controller is named as a co-executor of the Will along with his brother. Although they have equal legal power in making decisions regarding the estate, The Controller always wants to get his way. In this example, the estate includes Mom's house. The Controller wishes to sell the home because he feels it is best for the estate to have the money in the bank as opposed to the real estate. He strongly resists his co-executor's argument that the value of real estate is rising and that a sale may be premature. Unless the co-executor gives in to The Controller, the estate will be at a standstill and may require a court to intervene.

Suppose that The Controller is the sole executor. The Controller disregards the beneficiaries' requests that the home be kept. Those requests reflect their childhood memories of the home, which has been in the family for two generations. The Controller's response to the beneficiaries is: "Mom put me in charge. I know best."

Let's look at the other side of the coin. In Mom's Will, The Controller was not named as an executor. Here, even though he has no legal power under the Will to make decisions, he will still seek to impose his views on the executor. He may do this by demanding to be advised of every potential decision. He will be scrutinizing every move the executor makes and will be looking for any way to remove and replace the executor.

b)   The Aggressive One

Overlapping the personality of The Controller is that of the Aggressive One. Although this character may not be empowered by legal authority, he or she still does all he or she can to fulfil his or her own wishes through aggressive means. As soon as Dad dies, he may rush over to Dad's home. In that way, he will be the first through the door to take the pictures off the wall in Dad's home, even before his funeral. Other times, he mirrors the school yard bully, displaying his temper wherever necessary, through yelling, threats, insults and intimidation. Like The Controller, he wants his own way. The Aggressive One wants to create fear so that his opponents give up all or most of what the Aggressive One wishes to take.

Is either of the personalities we described above indicative of your brother or sister? If so, then how do you deal with them? In dealing with your controlling or aggressive sibling in an estate, you may consider the following approaches:

- Try to give some, but not absolute, control to him. In the case of The Controller, he never likes to be told what he must do. Involving him in the process is important. Requesting his opinion on decisions is one way to give him the feeling that he has some control.

- If you present logical and reasonable suggestions to your opponent, he has only two options: either agree with you, or reject your reasonable suggestions. Bear in mind that if you present reasonable suggestions to your opponent in writing, and he accepts them, you win. If he rejects these written reasonable suggestions, you have the beginning of a paper trail that a court will be able to follow. Your sibling's rejection of your reasonable proposal will reflect badly on him in court.

- The more unreasonable your sibling is, the more reasonable you should be. This means documenting the exchanges between you and your sibling as much as possible, bearing in mind that judges like reasonable people and dislike unreasonable ones. In some cases, where there is a clear contrast between your reasonable position and your sibling's unreasonable one, the day may come when even your sibling's own lawyer will advise him or her to yield to you to avoid losing in court.

- Never yield to the temptation to be unreasonable yourself. Don't let your emotions override sound judgment.

- If you are an executor faced with a beneficiary who is an Aggressive One or a Controller, it is important to keep very detailed records and respond to his or her communications within a reasonable time. The executor should avoid "cutting corners." Even though he may be your sibling, you should treat him like a person with whom you are doing business.

- Where you suspect that the Aggressive One is going to enter Mom's home to remove personal items, there are some pre-emptive steps you may consider. You may want to put valuables into storage, change the locks, hire a security guard, or at least notify the entire family that no one should enter Mom's home until her estate is settled.

c)   The Victim

Where there is an Aggressive One or a Controller, there is usually a Victim, who bears the brunt of such conduct. In many families, the Victim is often the younger sibling, who was never able to stand up to her more aggressive siblings. The Victim's desires were often overshadowed by her dominant siblings. For example, when the family ordered pizza, the Aggressive One got the toppings he wanted. The Victim was forced to eat the pizza with the toppings that her siblings wanted, or else eat none at all.

In a Family War, The Victim is often taken advantage of and may come away from the estate with less than he or she is entitled to. The Victim may not be willing to stand up to his or her siblings and fight.

d)   The Preferred Child

He feels as if he is the only child Mom ever loved. He believes that because of his "special bond" with Mom, he should get her most prized possessions. He may assert claims to those possessions, even though Mom's Will does not refer to them.

e)   The Black Sheep

He never felt fully part of the family. For this reason, he may not be concerned about the effect of a Family War on his siblings and may be more willing to risk it all to get what he wants.

f)   The Peacemaker

The Peacemaker is often caught in the middle of a Family War. There is nothing more important to The Peacemaker than the family.

Our client was the only daughter in a family with three other brothers. Two of her brothers were Aggressive Ones. Her other brother was a Victim. She found herself embroiled in a bitter family dispute after the death of her mother.

Our client understood the points of view of each of her brothers. She knew what caused their flashes of anger; knew intimately the gaps in their memories; and knew when and how to fill in those gaps. She was able to bring to life happier times from their collective youth, both with her descriptions and with the photographs that she shared with them.

Among the many skilful steps she took was to suggest to all of her brothers that their issues be dealt with internally and that all in-laws, including their wives, be barred from dealing with any estate matters. She had earned the respect of her brothers, and they agreed to follow her advice on many points. They listened to her, even though there remained areas where they disagreed. What she managed to do was to turn their minds to the value of a family relationship. She was able to draw to their attention that a fight would not only have a monetary cost, but a heavier price as well, being the loss of family. She made it clear to them that a fight might result in a new generation growing up without the bond that a family should have. She imparted to them the value of "us" as opposed to "me." She reminded her brothers that Mom would have been horrified to see her children fighting amongst themselves.

She was able to show her brothers that each had a point and that there are at least two sides to every story. She was able to defuse some of their feelings of anger by blaming the "system," instead of one brother blaming another.

What she was able to accomplish was to change an altercation that was destined for court into a manageable compromise. Without her involvement, the fight between her brothers would likely have pushed them apart and destroyed the family.

Not every estate dispute can be resolved by a Peacemaker. Sometimes The Controller or the Aggressive One will not listen to The Peacemaker because he or she is in the way of what they want.

The Peacemaker is used to dealing with anger from his or her siblings. He or she knows what it's like to be caught in the middle. He or she may not like the role, but it is something he or she has done all his or her life and feels that he or she is doing it in the best interests of the family.

One final note of caution: Although you think you really know your siblings, you may be wrong. For example, The Victim with the support of his or her lawyer may have developed a backbone. In this final battle, he or she may fight back. The Aggressive One may run out of steam because he or she has underestimated the draining nature of estate litigation. You may have been counting on The Peacemaker to intercede. However, he or she may feel that he or she has done enough during Mom's lifetime. Although intimate knowledge of your siblings can help, we offer the following words of caution: Do not base your whole strategy on what you expect your sibling to do.

CHAPTER 6

STRATEGIES TO PREVENT ESTATE LITIGATION

What can you do to head off a Family War before it happens? There are strategies that can be implemented both before and after the parent's death to minimize the risk or effect of a Family War.

1.   *BEFORE DEATH STRATEGIES- WHAT PARENTS CAN DO*

There is no substitute for good planning. A properly drafted Will and Powers of Attorney go a long way in avoiding a family fight.

Most parents know their children. They can often predict which child is going to cause a fight. They may want to take steps to protect their other "innocent" children in case that child starts a fight over their Will.

What can parents do to reduce the likelihood of an estate fight after their death? How can they protect their "innocent" children?

Let us take the example of a widow with two sons and a daughter. She is close to her younger son Bob and her daughter Mary, but is estranged from her eldest son Charles. Charles married a wealthy woman, who persuaded him that Mom was "evil." Before long, Mom and the other two children became convinced that Charles fell under the "spell" of his wife. Harsh words were exchanged among all concerned, and now Charles and his family have nothing to do with his siblings or Mom.

Mom wants to cut Charles out of her Will, but she expects that he and his wife will challenge her Will when she dies. She does not want to put her other children through the agony of a bitter estate dispute. What can Mom do to prevent this from happening while she is still capable of organizing and managing her affairs?

a)   Gift Assets

This strategy is the most dangerous. However, with the proper advice and in the right circumstances, it may have its benefits. Mom could give away substantial assets to Bob and Mary before she dies. Mom could either give the assets away to her children or put her children on title with her as joint owners. If she adds Bob and Mary as joint owners to her assets, they would receive those assets automatically upon Mom's death. Those assets would not form part of Mom's estate and would not be dealt with under her Will.

Mom should see a lawyer, who can properly document her intentions. The lawyer will confirm that Mom understood what she was doing and that that the transfers she made to Bob and Mary were actually intended as gifts.

If she puts the bulk of her assets in joint names with Bob and Mary, there would be very little left in her estate when she dies. Those assets will go to Bob and Mary regardless of what Mom's Will says. Charles will know that even if he successfully challenges the Will, he will not be entitled to the assets that Mom put in joint names with Bob and Mary. As a result, it may not be worth it for Charles to challenge the Will. Even if Charles won the Will challenge, what would he get? Very little.

However, Charles could still challenge Mom's transfer of ownership into joint names with Bob and Mary. As we have discussed, this type of challenge may be harder to win than a Will challenge.

Here is another potential advantage of Mom's transfer of her assets to Bob and Mary before she dies. In a Will challenge, the money is tied up until the fight is over. This means that Bob and Mary may not be able to use Mom's money to hire a lawyer. If the money is given to them before death, they may be able to use that money to hire a lawyer and put them on even footing with Charles and his wealthy family.

This strategy of gifting assets to Bob and Mary before death only works if:

- there is a loving, trusting and close relationship with Bob and Mary;

- Mom will never require these assets for her own support or needs; and

- she understands that she will never get those assets back without Bob and Mary's consent.

Mom should ensure that she is aware of any possible income tax implications in making the gifts to Bob and Mary. In addition, it should be noted that there are a number of significant risks in making these gifts. These include the possibility that Bob and Mary's spouses may get a share of the gifted assets if they separate or divorce. If either of the children have creditors, those creditors could attack any assets that Mom owns with Bob and Mary as joint owners. Mom would be very well advised to obtain legal and accounting advice before embarking on this strategy.

Once again, we emphasize that this strategy is very dangerous and that Mom should be very careful before giving away her assets or transferring them to Bob and Mary as joint owners.

b)   Videotape

Mom's lawyer advises her that a videotaped Will is not legal. He explains to her that a Will must be in writing. However, what he does explain is the role that videotaping may play in preventing challenges to her mental capacity.

The lawyer suggests that videotaping may make it more difficult, psychologically and legally, to challenge a Will. It may be easier for Charles to say, "Mom didn't know what she was doing" when he doesn't actually see Mom on videotape speaking about her intentions. Without this evidence, a challenger may be able to create all kinds of imaginary scenarios about what was going on in Mom's mind or what she understood or didn't understand. With videotape, there is less room for imagination

Her lawyer also explains that videotaping is not for everyone. While it sounds like a good idea, it may have many negative effects. The videotape will be carefully scrutinized by Charles's hostile eyes, looking for evidence to support his claim that Mom lacked mental capacity or was subjected to undue influence. The videotape may display the Will-maker's nervousness or her inordinately long pauses. She might display facial expressions that deviate from the way she looked in photographs or home videos. Mispronunciation, unusual phrasing, forgotten names, shifting of the eyes, fidgeting, nail biting or other mannerisms may give ammunition to Charles, who is seeking to challenge Mom's mental capacity.

Some lawyers do not recommend videotaping for these reasons. However, in some circumstances, it may be a prudent strategy to help protect the Will in case of attack.

c)   Prepare Evidence

Whatever takes place at the time of the signing of Mom's Will is very important and should be documented. Bearing in mind the possibility that Charles might be attacking her capacity to make a Will, Mom should ensure that certain precautions are put in place. These will serve as powerful barriers to Charles's possible attack.

- When Mom meets with her lawyer, she should make sure that Bob and Mary are not at that meeting;

- Mom should prepare for the meeting with her lawyer by reviewing her financial information, so that she knows what assets she has and what her estate is worth. She should be prepared to discuss in detail with her lawyer the reasons for excluding Charles;

- Mom should confirm with her lawyer that he is making careful notes of his discussions with her. For example, the lawyer's notes should show that Mom is well aware of her financial affairs, and that her intentions are very clear as to who should benefit from her estate and who should be excluded;

- If she is comfortable in discussing her Will with certain friends, she should tell them what she is doing in her Will and why. Specifically, the purpose of such discussions is to share with them her reasons for excluding Charles. Her friends will be able to serve as witnesses to show that Mom had made up her own mind and was not influenced by Bob and Mary. Her friends can also be another source of evidence that Mom's mental capacity was intact at the time she made her Will.

d)   Hold a Family Meeting

In some families, a meeting involving parents and children and, in some cases, in-laws, can avoid problems when the parents are gone. In many cases, what causes problems is the unexpected. Many lawsuits start when one child doesn't get what he or she expected in a Will. Even among close families, a lack of openness can cause problems.

One of Mom's assets happens to be her lakefront cottage, where Bob and Mary spent many vacations and long weekends. As the years passed, Mary became the primary user of the cottage, while Bob tended to be there less frequently. Mom's preliminary impression is to leave the cottage to Mary in her Will and to compensate Bob with an extra cash gift to even out their interests in her estate.

Would a family meeting be helpful in dealing with the issue of the cottage? There may be aspects to the situation that lie beyond even Mom's observations and impressions.

For example, Mom may be wrong to assume that Mary cares more about the cottage than Bob does. It is true that Bob uses the cottage more sporadically than Mary does, but that does not change the fact that Bob looks upon the cottage as the "family cottage." He has a strong emotional attachment to the cottage because of the years he spent there as a child.

What will happen when Bob finds out that Mom left the cottage to Mary and that he will only be able to visit the cottage when he is invited by Mary? Will he feel hurt and disappointed? Will the money he receives compensate him adequately? Will he or his spouse or children feel "cut out"?

What if Mom is unaware that Mary needs more of a financial boost than Mom imagined, and that it would have been preferable to have given the extra cash to Mary and the cottage to Bob? What if both children would have been content to share the cottage and now this is not an option?

Mom would prefer to procrastinate and sweep these issues under the rug, to be dealt with at "another time" or "a better time" or "later."

However, a family meeting allows Mom and the children to raise all of the questions while the cottage is still in Mom's name and while she is still there to help her children deal with these issues. The reality is that the children will eventually have to deal with the types of problems we are discussing.

Is it better to leave a legacy of problems for the children? What if Mom guessed wrong about what her children wanted and how they felt? Will Bob and Mary be forced into a business-like transaction involving lawyers to resolve the cottage issue?

A family meeting would have likely exposed Bob and Mary's feelings towards the cottage. It would have given each participant an opportunity to raise concerns and to discuss ways of working through the potential problems surrounding the "family" cottage. Later, when Mom dies and her Will is read, neither child is surprised about what happened to the cottage. In the world of estates, surprise is rarely a good thing.

e)   Insert Protective Clauses in the Will

If a dispute is expected, there are some clauses that can be added to the Will that can discourage litigation.

Mom fully expects that Charles is going to challenge her Will. She asks her lawyer whether it would be a good idea to leave him something rather than cutting him out completely.

Mom realizes that if she leaves a gift to Charles in her Will he may be reluctant to attack the Will if he knew that such an attack would deprive him of that gift. In many jurisdictions, Mom can have her lawyer insert a special clause in her Will that may have this effect. The clause will say that if Charles challenges the Will and loses, he also loses his entitlement to any gifts under the Will.

If Charles challenges Mom's Will and loses, instead of getting a small share in the estate, he gets nothing. It makes a Will challenge an "All or Nothing" lawsuit. Mom has to make sure that the amount of the gift to Charles is big enough to discourage him from taking the risk of losing it. Charles may be hesitant to launch a frivolous lawsuit against Mom's estate because he knows that if he loses the lawsuit, he loses everything. This type of clause is not valid in every jurisdiction. Even if it is valid, it must be drafted with precision in order to be accepted by a court.

In addition to protecting the Will, there are clauses that can protect an executor from attacks by the beneficiaries.

Let's assume that Mom decides to leave Charles a share of the estate, but names Bob and Mary as the executors. She may be concerned that Charles will make trouble for Bob and Mary. You will recall that we discussed a number of claims that beneficiaries can make against an executor. How can Mom protect Bob and Mary from Charles's attacks?

157

An "exoneration" clause inserted in the Will may protect the executor from frivolous or unjustified attacks from the beneficiaries. An exoneration clause will typically provide that the executor is protected from any claim made against him or her as long as he or she has acted in good faith. Accordingly, he or she is protected from many types of beneficiary's attacks. The legal costs of his or her defence will be paid out of the estate monies, not out of his or her own pocket.

In our example, Bob and Mary are executors of Mom's estate. Mom owned shares in various companies. Bob and Mary decide to sell the shares right after Mom's death. A few weeks later, those shares significantly rise in value. Of course, Bob and Mary did not know those shares were going to increase in value, they were just trying to settle the estate as soon as possible. However, if Charles is a beneficiary, he may decide to sue Bob and Mary. He may claim that they should reimburse the estate for the value that the estate would have received if Bob and Mary had waited before selling the shares. Whether you believe this is a frivolous claim or not, Bob and Mary will still have to defend themselves. During that litigation, Bob and Mary decide to settle with Charles to end the litigation. To get it over with, and because their lawyer advises them that it's not a clear-cut case, they agree to pay their own legal fees. Had Mom included an exoneration clause in her Will, Bob and Mary may have been better protected from Charles' attack.

f)   Give an Explanation

Assuming that Mom decides not to leave anything to Charles, she should make the reasons for her decision as clear as possible.

One way for her to do this is to include an explanation in her Will, setting out her reasons for cutting Charles out. For example, Mom may include a clause in her Will that states, "I have deliberately not included my son Charles in my Will because I do not have any relationship with him."

The insertion of Mom's reasoning for disinheriting Charles creates very serious obstacles for him. It will be difficult for him to argue that the Will did not express her true intentions due to undue influence, oversight or incapacity.

One word of caution, however, before endorsing this type of protection as some form of "cure-all": It is crucial that the Will be updated to reflect any changes in Mom's relationship with Charles. If her relationship with Charles improves, the clause will be seen by Charles as outdated and unreflective of the warming of her relationship with him. As we have seen, feelings that the Will does not reflect what Mom really wanted can lead to estate fights. Thus an outdated Will with this type of clause gives Charles the motivation to challenge the Will on that basis.

There is also cause for concern where the explanation is very specific, for example, "I am excluding Charles because he stole money from me." It turns out that Mom wrongly believed that Charles stole money. In fact, it was the housekeeper that stole the money. This gives Charles ammunition to challenge Mom's mental capacity in making the Will.

Another option is for Mom to include the explanation in a letter to accompany the Will, rather than putting it in the Will itself. The letter should explain Mom's reasons for cutting Charles out of the Will. One advantage of this form of expression is that Mom can set out her explanation in far more detail than she can in her Will. She can express her feelings in detail and provide examples of Charles's estrangement. Another advantage is that the letter will likely not become a public document when she dies. On the other hand, her Will may become a public document when Mom dies.

g)   Get Proper Legal Advice

To reduce the likelihood of a challenge to your Will, it is prudent to have your Will drafted by a Wills lawyer, who will be familiar with the laws, procedures and formalities involved in drafting a Will.

If you are in the process of preparing your Will and you see the warning signs of oncoming conflict, you should share your concerns with your Wills lawyer.

In the event that your Will is challenged, your Wills lawyer will likely be called as a witness to testify as to your mental capacity.

In Mom's case, she has decided to cut Charles out of her Will. That Will is going to be very unwelcome to him. He might be tempted to challenge the Will on the grounds that, because of Mom's age, she lacked the necessary mental capacity to make the Will. If a lawyer prepared and witnessed her Will, he would be a prime witness to verify Mom's mental capacity at the time of making and signing her Will.

If she retained an experienced Wills lawyer with a good reputation, he may have more credibility with the Court in the event that he has to act as a witness to testify about Mom's mental capacity and intentions.

h)   Obtain a Mental Assessment

In a court challenge over the mental capacity of the Will-maker, some of the most important evidence will be medical evidence.

The value of obtaining such medical evidence is clear. Firstly, as a person ages or as his or her health declines, opportunities arise where others might observe incidents of his or her indecision, hesitation, forgetfulness or other similar actions. The Will challenger might take advantage of such observations to support his or her case.

In Mom's case, a letter from her personal doctor who knows her well may be enough. Her doctor can testify about his or her observations, examinations and findings regarding Mom's mental capacity.

When she sees her Wills lawyer, he suggests that because of her age, the size of her estate, and the fact that she is cutting out one of her three children, a simple doctor's letter may not be enough. Also, Mom's personal doctor retired last year and a new doctor took over his practice. Mom has only seen him once. In these circumstances, Mom's lawyer recommends that she undergo a full mental capacity assessment. If Charles does attack Mom's Will, Bob and Mary will have to defend the Will. This assessment will give Bob and Mary more ammunition to fight off Charles.

It is important to add that the doctor's assessment or observations should be made close in time to the signing of the Will.

What happens if a Will is challenged and there is no medical evidence of the Will-maker's mental capacity at the time he or she made the Will? The court will have to rely on evidence of non-medical witnesses, who will testify as to their own observations. One of the Will-maker's friends may have observed him calling his son by the wrong name. Another person might recall that the Will-maker was very alert, had a good memory, and was up-to-date on world affairs.

In many circumstances, these conflicting observations by non-medical witnesses would be outweighed by proper medical evidence.

i)   Give a Gift Directly to your Grandchildren

Mom has decided to exclude her son Charles from her Will. What will discourage Charles from challenging the Will? Perhaps if Mom gives a gift in the Will to Charles's own children, he may be less likely to challenge the Will.

If Charles is successful in setting aside Mom's Will, he will have deprived his own children of the gift that their grandmother left them. Even if he isn't successful, the costs to the estate of the challenge could reduce his own children's inheritance.

By utilizing this strategy, Mom has put Charles in a conflict, in essence pitting him against his own children. In other words, the price that Charles must pay in order to challenge the Will is to place himself in a conflict with his own children by depriving them of the gift left by their grandmother.

2.   AFTER DEATH STRATEGIES – WHAT CHILDREN CAN DO

We have examined what Mom can do before she dies if she expects a Family War to break out after her death. Assuming that Mom has now passed away, she can no longer minimize or prevent conflict among her children: what is done is done. The burden of dealing with potential conflict is now left to those who survive her.

As we have seen, many estates have the potential for creating a Family War. However, there are strategies that you can use to minimize the risk that your parent's estate will end up destroying your relationship with your siblings.

Let's examine some strategies that may help you and your family avoid inheriting turmoil when your parents pass away.

a)   Deal with Immediate Issues First and Leave Other Matters for Later

Regardless of the possibility of disagreement, you must still deal with urgent matters, such as the funeral and burial, first.

Heightened emotions swirl around during the period of mourning. It is wise to recognize that bitter words may be uttered that ought not to be said. The source of such bitter words may be due to feelings of hurt and pain at the loss of a parent, rather than from hostile intent. This may be the time to give the benefit of the doubt to siblings if they say offensive things to you. If possible, try and avoid the impulse to respond in kind, which will only add fuel to the fire.

If you are executor: although you have the final say over Mom's funeral and burial, it may help to ease tensions if you ask your siblings for their input as to funeral and burial arrangements. Making them feel included at this emotionally sensitive time may be a soothing influence when later a fight looms over the administration or distribution of the estate.

After those immediate issues are dealt with, it would be preferable to deal next with non-controversial issues, those with an easy resolution, or a low risk of hostility. This helps to build a bridge between you and your siblings, creating trust and momentum towards a good working relationship. Also, when you do get to the controversial issues, you have at least made progress in moving the estate forward. For example, in Mom's case, Charles would like some photographs from the family home. In order to establish some form of communication, perhaps Bob and Mary will agree to make copies of the photographs for Charles. Similarly, perhaps everyone can agree that Mom's old clothes can be given to charity.

b)   Find out Your Legal Rights

In defusing what appears to be looming hostility, the first step is to know where you stand legally. For example, a person claims to be the deceased's dependant and wants a bigger share of the estate. While you may believe that his claim is totally without merit, you should speak to your lawyer. The lawyer may advise you that under the law, that person has a legitimate claim. That being the case, what would have been the point of engaging in a harsh exchange with the claimant, elevating the hostility, only to be forced, at the expense of the estate, to back down later?

On the other hand, you may be the one who wishes to advance a claim against the estate. There is little point in making idle threats, devoid of any legal basis.

For example, assume your wife died last year and her mother just passed away without a Will. You were very close to your mother-in-law and she treated you almost like her own child. You feel that you should be entitled to a share of her estate. You believe that your brothers-in-law are going to rip you off by not giving you what you feel you are entitled to from your mother-in-law's estate. You write a hostile letter to them and are ready to deliver it. You should pause before sending that letter and seek legal advice. Why?

After seeing your lawyer, you find out that you have no legal right to any share of your mother-in-law's estate. The only way you can get anything is if your brothers-in-law decide, in the spirit of "good will," to voluntarily share it with you. If you send the letter you will, no doubt, guarantee that they will give you nothing. In fact, those baseless threats to your brothers-in-law about a lawsuit may only serve to destroy your relationship with them. You will never be entitled to anything under the law. After being informed of your legal rights, you decide that a better strategy would be to contact your brothers-in-law and discuss your feelings with them on a friendly, rather than a confrontational, basis.

Finally, remember that some of your rights are limited by time. Depending on where you live, there may be a Statute of Limitations which gives a party only so much time to initiate a proceeding.

Without knowing the applicable law, you might lose a valid claim or be unaware of a valid defence.

c) Communicate

Now that you know where you stand legally, you should next consider how to communicate your position to your siblings.

The first question is whether or not to use a lawyer to initiate communication with your sibling. There are times when it may be better to express what you need to say to a sibling, without the involvement of legal counsel. A sibling may be more receptive to your proposal if you communicate personally with him rather than through a lawyer. That does not mean that you shouldn't obtain legal advice before presenting your proposal — your lawyer can guide you on the important legal issues and, most importantly, advise you on what *not* to say to your sibling.

In many circumstances, however, personal direct communication between siblings in a family dispute is not productive and may often make the situation worse. What you say could be used against you by your sibling if the matter goes to court. Your lawyer will be careful not to prejudice your position and will ensure that your rights are protected.

Involving a lawyer to communicate your position to the other side is a major decision. Once the lawyers are involved, it is no longer an internal family matter; it is now a legal dispute. Emotionally, it will be next to impossible to turn back the clock to the time before that first lawyer's letter was received.

Where both sides have a mutual intention to communicate, there may be some hope of avoiding legal warfare. However, if only one side is open to communication and the other is not, the parties may have no choice but to resort to lawyers and the legal process.

d)   Encourage the Trouble-Maker to get his own Lawyer

You have tried everything possible to communicate with your brother. You have come to the conclusion that he will not listen to reason, whether from you directly or from your lawyer.

The best thing that can happen to you, if your brother is being unreasonable, is for him to get his own lawyer. A lawyer may quickly point out to your brother that he is acting unreasonably and does not have a legal basis for a claim.

Many times, lawyers can help to soften positions and calm the participants. Because the lawyers have no emotional stake in the family dispute, they can help steer their clients away from the emotional issues and focus on the legal ones.

If your sibling thinks you are bluffing or being deceitful, invite your sibling to get his own legal advice on this point. You may even propose that the estate pay for his initial consultation with his lawyer. Having his own lawyer tell him that he is wrong is much more effective than you or your lawyer telling him he is wrong.

e)   Don't Gang Up

People don't like to feel threatened. If your opponent feels he is being ganged up on he may get defensive and dangerous. For example, if there are three children and two are ganging up on the third, the third child will likely become distrustful and defensive and may start pushing back.

Even though you and your siblings may be able to form a majority against your other sibling, this power should not be abused.

To begin with, put yourself in the position of the sibling in the minority. How would you feel in his position? If the majority attempts to establish dialogue with him, extending every opportunity to resolve the issues on a reasonable basis, there is a possibility that at least some of the issues in dispute might be resolved. His feelings of anger and being victimized might be defused.

Contrast this with the situation where the majority refuses to empathize with the sibling in the minority, and attempts to bully him into submission, or force concessions from him. The majority does so at its peril. The sibling in the minority may, out of a fight or flight instinct:

> a) hire a lawyer and fight fire with fire. The result may be a long, bitter and costly estate battle that escalates; or

> b) yield to the pressures of the moment. However, that sibling may be left with bitter feelings that can have a corrosive effect on the family relationship forever.

f)   Involve Friends and Family

Caution must be exercised in considering the possibility of involving family members or friends, who up to this point are not actively involved in the dispute between you and your siblings.

If there is an upside to the involvement of such third parties, it may take this form:

Imagine your uncle, who is seen by all as neutral and level headed. He has the respect of both you and your sibling, with whom you are fighting. He can see that your position is fair and reasonable. Your uncle also feels that your sibling is acting unreasonably and will end up hurting himself and destroying the family if he persists in continuing his battle against you.

Perhaps your uncle would undertake to keep the family from splitting apart even further by agreeing to have a private talk with your unreasonable sibling. He can bring into perspective certain realities that your sibling may be overlooking. Your uncle might remind him about how close you were in the past. He may enlighten him about how the future might look after a Family War has been fought—having to cross the room at a family wedding to avoid you. Hearing his uncle tell him how Dad would be "turning over in his grave" if he could see his children fighting can have a powerful impact. Your uncle has the capacity to create many such emotional photographs: images once imprinted may be slow to leave your sibling's mind. Your uncle may put the entire dispute into a much deeper and more meaningful background. He may be able to restore a perspective that had been buried by the frictions of the day.

Unfortunately, involvement of family and friends in this fashion requires careful consideration. Despite all the benefits that we have just expressed, there may be reasons not to involve family and friends in this way:

- Your uncle, as respected as he may be, is not your lawyer. Therefore, nothing you tell him is protected by lawyer-client privilege. Your brother can subpoena your uncle as a witness to force him to disclose to the court everything that you told your uncle in confidence;

- Unless your uncle is a trained mediator, he will not necessarily be able to deal with negative comments that you confide in him, the way a mediator might;

- Your uncle, no matter how sympathetic and understanding he may be, could be drawn into the battle. He might even change sides, unexpectedly, becoming supportive of your sibling. He may repeat what you confided in him. This could set you up for a possible slander claim from your sibling;

- Your uncle might not grasp the subtler points of your side of the argument. He could misunderstand the essential points you are trying to make. He may not make notes of what you are trying to express and, as a result, could miscommunicate your position to your sibling. Instead of clarifying matters, his own confusion may add fuel to the fire. Furthermore, if he does make notes, they might be subject to disclosure in the litigation;

- Your uncle may make your sibling feel that the family is "ganging-up" on him, intensifying your sibling's feeling of isolation from the family. This may increase his defensiveness, creating a barrier to the settlement of the family dispute.

In the end, involving a family member or friend could be a powerful instrument that can result in a quick settlement. However, you must balance this potential benefit against the risk that your strategy might backfire.

g)   Give up Non-Essential Points

If a particular issue is very important for your sibling, but not as important for you, consider conceding that issue.

Imagine that you are named as executor and your brother is not. He is very upset. He feels slighted because he believes that he has constantly been overlooked by your parents, and his skills and life experience were never recognized by them. His anger is expressed in a challenge to the Will, which will seriously and adversely affect what would have been a routine estate administration.

If, in this case, being an executor is very important to your brother, and not as important to you, then it would make sense to resolve that issue.   This could avert a serious fight. With this in mind, in order to pacify your brother, you could suggest to him that you will resign as executor, so that neither you nor your brother is in control of the estate. You suggest to him that you both agree to appoint a bank or other neutral party to act as the executor. With this concession, you have validated your brother's feelings. What would have become a devastating situation is now defused.

h)   Come Up with a "Neutral" Solution

For most problems, there may be more than one solution. For example, imagine that Mom's Will leaves all of the household items to be divided equally among the three children, now that Dad has already passed away. Dividing parents' personal effects is one of the leading causes of arguments among children after the parents are gone. How do the children decide who gets what items?

There are strategies available which are neutral and fair to all of the children. Let's look at four simple suggestions, which can help avoid, or at least minimize, arguments over the distribution of personal effects.

A.   Picking Lots

One option consists of dividing all of the personal effects into several relatively equal groups. For example, one set of dishes, one set of silverware and one of the paintings form one "lot." Another set of dishes, silverware and another painting form the second lot. One lot is set up for each child. They are labelled as lots 1, 2, and so forth. Corresponding numbered cards are put into a container. Each of the children draws one of the cards and takes the lot that corresponds to the number.

B.   Auction

When the children cannot agree on how a particular item should be distributed, an auction process can be used. Each child who wishes to have that item puts a bid in a sealed envelope. When the envelopes are opened, the highest bid takes the item. The proceeds are paid to the estate. If the item is very expensive, the payment can be made by way of deduction against the bidder's share of the estate.

C.   Purchase of Assets

Every personal effect is appraised, given a price, and sold to the children. The proceeds are paid to the estate. If no one wishes to purchase an item, it can be sold to a third party and the proceeds paid to the estate. If two or more children desire the same item, they can use the auction procedure referred to above.

D.   Rotating the Selection

One of the most common options is to have each child pick one item in rotation. To make it fair, the order is reversed in the next round — the child who picked last in the first round picks first in the second round. The original order can be selected by picking straws. The order should be fixed on a random basis, not based on something such as birth order. Otherwise, the order is not neutral and may create resentment.

What is common to all four suggestions is neutrality. From neutrality comes a feeling of fairness. From a feeling of fairness comes acceptance.

i)   Use a Neutral Mediator

Because of family history, traditional roles in the family and the heightened emotion of estate disputes, neutral parties are often very helpful in settling differences early on.

Mediation is one way of involving a neutral party to assist in resolving estate fights.

A mediation is a formal meeting with a neutral person facilitating the discussions.

In mediations, all of the parties are present, along with their lawyers. Sometimes, the parties will meet in the same room together. Other times, each of the parties has his or her own room. The mediator will shuffle from one room to another to involve the different parties. In most jurisdictions, everything said at a mediation is confidential. This means that the parties can be completely open about settlement, knowing that what they say cannot be used against them in court.

The mediator is a trained facilitator experienced in resolving disputes. He or she helps the parties reach their own agreement. A mediator does not decide who is right or wrong or which side "wins." The mediator can only make suggestions for resolving the issues.

The benefit is that the mediator has special skill in removing many of the "side" issues and concentrating on getting to the most important issues.   The mediator is neutral and does not take sides. Instead, the mediator will move between the parties, explaining one party's concerns to the other party and vice-versa. The mediator will know what both sides want from the other and what may work to bring the sides closer to a settlement.

One great benefit of mediation is an opportunity for the parties to "have their say." Because most estate litigation cases settle before trial, many times the parties never get their "day in court." At the mediation, you can express your feelings about the situation, about how you feel about your sibling and what he or she has done, about what is fair, and what Mom really wanted. You will have an opportunity to express these feelings to a neutral party, who can then pass them on to your siblings. At the very least, at the end of the mediation you will feel that you have had a chance to "have your say."

Sometimes the parties can agree to go to mediation early on in the dispute. This can be important because once a lawsuit is started accusations and allegations start to fly. This makes settlement even harder to achieve. If mediation can be held before that occurs, there is a greater chance of settling the dispute and avoiding a full-blown Family War.

In some jurisdictions, mediation is mandatory. In these jurisdictions, once estate litigation begins all of the parties are required to attend a mediation session. Check with your lawyer to see if that is the case where you live.

j)   Be Reasonable

Judges like to help reasonable people and punish unreasonable ones. In estate litigation, judges usually can find a way to help the party who is being reasonable. As we have said before, some of the best advice in estate litigation is "the more unreasonable they are, the more reasonable you should be."

Being reasonable when your brother is being unreasonable may not be easy. It is much easier to "fight fire with fire" and be unreasonable back to him. But remember, your brother's lawyer will try and turn every little unreasonable action you take into a major issue.

Experienced judges know that emotion plays a big part in estate litigation. If they get the feeling that one party is fighting out of spite or out of emotion, even if that party has a valid legal claim, judges will view his or her position more suspiciously. Being unreasonable is often a sign that something other than a legitimate legal position is behind the litigation.

Everything you do should be done in the most objective and dispassionate manner possible. For example, a brother and sister were fighting over their father's estate. The sister was being completely unreasonable throughout the whole litigation. It was very difficult for the brother to remain reasonable when the sister was being so difficult, but he did. That is, until the trial. At a crucial point in the trial, the sister gave evidence which so upset her brother that he stood up and shouted in open court, "Dad didn't want you to get as much as me because he knew you were a lesbian!" It was clear that the judge recognized how painful that statement was to the sister and why the sister was fighting so hard. She was fighting for acceptance in the family. Immediately, the judge knew that the brother was as much at fault as the sister for the litigation.

k)   Agree to Change Mom's Will

There are times when everyone in the family is determined to bring about a fair result that pleases all of them. The only problem is that Mom's Will distributes her estate in a way that is different from what the family wants. Using the earlier example, assume Mom cut Charles out of her Will. When they find out about the Will after Mom dies, Bob and Mary may feel that it was not right that Charles was cut out of Mom's Will. They may want to try and re-establish their relationship with him and his children.

In many jurisdictions, the law will allow all of the beneficiaries to make a legal agreement to vary the distribution contained in a Will.

Bob and Mary could agree to an arrangement where Charles gets a share of Mom's estate even though Mom's Will did not include him.

There are a number of legal formalities for this kind of arrangement to be effective, including:

1. All adult beneficiaries must consent to the arrangement. Assuming Bob and Mary are the only two beneficiaries under Mom's Will, both would have to agree.

2. There must not be any children under the age of majority with actual or potential rights of inheritance to the estate. Had Mom named Charles's minor children as beneficiaries, they could not legally agree to change Mom's Will. This is because, under the law of most jurisdictions, minor children are not allowed to make a contract.

3. There must be no party who is mentally incapable. If either Bob or Mary is mentally incapable at the time Mom dies, the mentally incapable child would not be able to consent to the arrangement.

If everyone agrees to the arrangement changing Mom's Will, it is important that each party obtains separate independent legal advice before signing the agreement.

CHAPTER 7

IMPROVING YOUR CHANCES IN AN ESTATE DISPUTE

1. Taking a Business Approach to Estate Disputes - It May All Boil Down to Money

Although there may be many non-financial issues driving a family fight, at the end of the day money is often the yard stick for success in estate litigation. A court cannot resolve all of the emotional issues in the family. If your objective in going to court is to see justice done as a matter of principle, you will likely be disappointed in what a court can do. In most estate litigation cases, all a court will do is award money or assets to one party or another. Therefore, to some of the participants, money will represent truth and justice.

If we are using the same premise as the one used in business, where money is the bottom line, let's take a look at a couple of strategies that might be helpful.

It must be remembered that legal rights, obligations and procedures may vary from one legal jurisdiction to another. In order to determine whether any of the following strategies can work in your jurisdiction, you will have to speak to your lawyer or tax professional.

Think of an estate as a pie. There are a number of ways to increase the amount of the pie that you get. One way is to make the pie bigger so that everyone gets a bigger slice. Another way is to minimize the amount being taken out of the pie by others.

a)   Enlarging the Pie: Strategies Designed to Increase Everyone's Share

The executor can increase the pie for the beneficiaries if he can bring assets, which appear to flow outside of the estate, back into the estate. If this is possible, the estate will grow larger.

One example may involve joint assets that the deceased held together with someone else. Parents often put assets into joint names with one or more of their children. As we have seen, sometimes it is done for convenience purposes only and is not meant as a gift. Let's assume that Mom had a bank account, which she held jointly with your brother. If you can show that Mom did not want that bank account to go to your brother on her death, the joint account will be brought back into the estate. If it is part of the estate, it will be divided according to Mom's Will. In that case, the value of the estate has just been increased by the amount of the bank account. The beneficiaries who share Mom's estate will each get a slice of a bigger pie.

A similar strategy can be applied to gifts made by a parent to a child during the parent's lifetime. Arguments based upon undue influence or mental incapacity might apply where an elderly parent gives a gift to one of his four children before he dies. The other children, for example, might be aware of evidence that the elderly parent was being treated for Alzheimer's or was being constantly threatened and harassed by the child who received the gift. If they successfully challenge that gift, the money must be returned to the estate to be divided among the beneficiaries who share in the parent's estate.

Both of these examples show how the pie can be enlarged, which in turn increases the size of each slice.

b) Keeping the Pie – Strategies Designed to Reduce Estate Expenses

As the saying goes, "There are only two sure things — death and taxes." Taxes can take a big chunk out of an estate. If there are ways to legitimately reduce the taxes that flow out of the estate, the size of the pie will be maintained.

There are many ways that taxes can be reduced in estate litigation. Proper tax advice may often result in significant savings of income or capital gains tax, to which an estate may be exposed. However, in order for an estate to benefit from such advice, a tax professional should be retained. Because each estate is different, your professional advisor will consider how to structure a settlement so that taxes are minimized. For example, certain assets may be taxed at a lower rate if given to certain beneficiaries. In some jurisdictions, gifts to the deceased's spouse may result in less tax having to be paid. You will want to ensure that any resolution maximizes the potential estate by reducing the tax payable.

This is one reason why settlement among all the parties is preferable to a court judgment. A court will not necessarily take into account strategies to minimize taxes when making a decision.

This book is not designed to offer specific tax advice. Because income tax laws are so complex, it is important to obtain professional advice on the legality of any type of settlement involving these issues.

Any practical discussion of reducing estate expenses involves the consideration of legal fees. When confronted with a sibling who is claiming against the estate, you have to expect to spend legal fees to defend your position. The costs of estate litigation are substantial. That is one advantage that a challenger has. He knows that if he starts a challenge, the estate will spend money defending it.

It may be that the best chance you have of keeping as much of your slice as possible is to stop the matter from proceeding to court. This way you can control some of the costs before they become unmanageable. In some cases, even winning the lawsuit in court may leave you with a smaller share than you would have received if you had settled earlier.

The consideration of settling with your opponent should be based upon a business-like decision, as opposed to being driven by emotion or principle. There is an old saying, "Sometimes a bad settlement is better than a good lawsuit."

2. **PRACTICAL SUGGESTIONS TO ENHANCE YOUR POSITION IN A FAMILY WAR**

a) **Help Your Lawyer**

To maximize your result in a Family War, you and your lawyer have to operate as a team. There are ways that you can help your lawyer make your case better.

At the outset of your relationship, remember that your lawyer knows nothing about your case. He will probably never know as much about the facts of your case as you do. In order for the lawyer to understand your case as quickly as possible, focus on the facts, not the emotion. He must know the facts as they are, for better or worse. If you exaggerate, or, worse yet, mislead your lawyer, you will suffer when your lawyer is caught off guard by the other side with the truth.

In explaining your case to your lawyer, state the facts in a way that is easy to understand. Begin with the main points. Try not to go off on tangents. As his or her grasp of the case deepens, the lawyer will prompt you for more details. If you feel he or she is missing a detail that you believe is important, it is your responsibility to fill in the blanks for him or her.

If anything new occurs, such as a meeting or a discussion with your siblings or potential witnesses, keep your lawyer up to date with a short phone call or brief letter or email.

To help your lawyer focus, there are two items of information that will be crucial to him or her:

a) a family tree; and
b) a written chronology of events.

Family Tree

The family tree will help the lawyer understand the various participants right from the start. It will also alert the lawyer to any parties who are not yet involved, but should be. For example, Mom's Will gives your brother a share of her estate in trust during his lifetime. When he dies, the Will says that his share goes to his children. It will be crucial for the lawyer to be aware of your brother's children, as well as their ages, in order to properly understand the case.

A sample family tree looks like this:

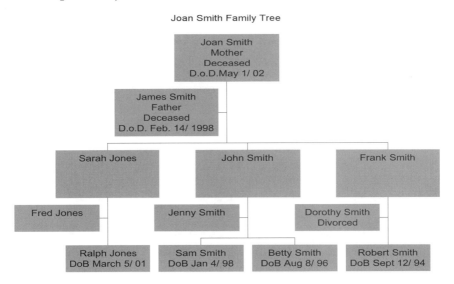

Assume that Joan Smith's Will is being challenged. Her daughter, Sarah Jones, is challenging the Will, while Sarah's two brothers, John and Frank, are defending the Will

From the family tree, the lawyer for Sarah Jones immediately understands who Sarah is fighting with and the possibility that Joan's grandchildren are under the age of 18. In some jurisdictions, this may result in a government lawyer having to be appointed to represent these minors, in the event that the dispute affects them. The family tree also shows that Sarah's Dad died before Sarah's Mom. This may be relevant to interpreting her mom's Will.

The lawyer will also use the family tree to assist in determining who must be served with the court documents.

The family tree will also be helpful when Sarah's lawyer is presenting her case to a judge or a mediator.

Chronology

The other important document that can help your lawyer understand your case is the chronology of events. The chronology should set out all important events in chronological order. The chronology should include, for example, the following information:

- Date of birth of the Deceased;

- Dates of marriage and divorce for all family members;

- The dates of all Wills that you know about;

- If mental capacity is in issue, the medical history of the deceased, including the dates of any hospital admissions or major illnesses such as strokes or heart attacks;

- The dates of death of any children or spouses;

- The dates when the deceased acquired any significant assets;

- The dates of any large gifts made by the deceased during his or her lifetime;

- The dates of any major family disagreements or estrangements; and

- The dates of any other facts that you believe are important, such as when the deceased went into a nursing home, etc.

The chronology should also refer to any important documents and the dates they were made.

Providing your lawyer with these documents will reduce the amount of time he or she will have to spend to obtain this information. This will likely reduce the amount of legal fees that you will have to spend at the beginning of the case.

Changing Lawyers

Sometimes your relationship with your lawyer may not go smoothly. You may at some point even consider changing your legal representation. However, before you do, there are some factors you should consider.

There are downsides to changing your lawyer in mid-stream. One major issue is that the new lawyer will have to learn the case from scratch. This will translate into additional expense to you and a delay in the progress of the case.

Worse yet, your change of legal representation may signal a weakness to your opponent. Perhaps the other side will form the impression that you fired your lawyer because he did not believe that you had a winning case. Perhaps changing your lawyer will confirm your opponent's impression that you are unreasonable and that even your lawyer cannot get along with you. This may make it more difficult to convince the other side to take your position seriously.

When you attempt to retain a new lawyer, you may find that he or she will question you very thoroughly. He or she will wonder why your relationship with the first lawyer broke down. The burden will be on you to convince the new lawyer that there was nothing sinister or negative in the breakdown between you and your first lawyer.

Certainly, these concerns could influence the attitude of the second lawyer regarding the payment of his or her fees. He or she may be suspicious that one of the reasons you had to change lawyers was because you couldn't afford the fees or you refused to pay. In order to protect him or herself, he or she may ask for a greater retainer up front. This will mean that you have to invest even more money in your case.

All of this leads to one conclusion: try to pick the right lawyer at the start of your case. Look for a lawyer who focuses on estate matters. Ask friends and relatives who have been through an estate case to recommend a lawyer. Contact your local Bar Association for names of estate lawyers in your area. Interview your prospective lawyer. Find out what experience he or she has in similar cases. Do you think you can work with this person through a very difficult time of your life? Find out how the lawyer expects to be paid. Does he or she charge on an hourly rate or on a contingency basis? How often will he or she bill you? Can you afford him or her?

b)   Be Guarded

A Family War can be just that—a very dirty fight. You must be on guard against providing any evidence that might be used against you. Specifically, you must be wary of providing your potential adversary with evidence that is going to help him or her. He or she will look for evidence to enhance his or her position.

Take this dramatic example:

You and your brother are writing up the obituary and preparing the eulogy for your father's funeral. Dad's live-in housekeeper diligently looked after him during the last years of his life. You and your brother appreciate all the care she provided for Dad. She was there every day. In addition to doing all the housework, she would keep Dad company at dinnertime, she took him shopping, and even spent some weekends with Dad so he wouldn't be alone. Because you and your brother lived out of town, she was the one who spent the most time with Dad.

You and your brother want to say all of this in the eulogy and mention her in the obituary.

It is sad to say that your well meaning comments may come back to haunt you. If your eulogy is not carefully worded, it may play into the hands of the housekeeper, whose intention may be to claim a share of Dad's estate. In thinking of how to word your eulogy, consider this possibility:

After Dad's death, you get a letter from the housekeeper's lawyer claiming that she was *much more* than a housekeeper to Dad. The lawyer claims that she should be entitled to half of Dad's estate. Her lawyer includes a tape recording of your eulogy. He suggests that you listen to your own words:

> "After Mom died, she stepped into Mom's shoes and brought life back to Dad."

> "Dad told us that the years she spent with him were some of the best times of his life."

> "She was like part of our family."

> "We don't know how to thank her."

You are shocked that your kind, heartfelt words are being used against you, but in a Family War this is what could happen.

The eulogy or obituary will not automatically win the case for the housekeeper, but it could be a valuable piece of evidence. The housekeeper will point out to a judge that your comments about her were made honestly and without concern about your legal position. Because you never expected a lawsuit, your own words may take you by surprise. If during the litigation you try and backtrack, saying you were just trying to be nice, a judge may not believe you.

That is not to say that you shouldn't have praised the housekeeper—she deserved praise. But be aware that a person intent on litigating will look for anything to win the Family War.

One final note: what happens at the funeral is often included as evidence in the estate battle. The funeral is supposed to be about respecting the memory of the deceased loved one. Unfortunately, often in estate disputes, the events surrounding the funeral are put under a microscope. A harsh word spoken or a confrontation at the funeral could end in an affidavit filed with the court. Also, parties may point to a family member's absence at the funeral as indicating a lack of love or a sign of disrespect for the deceased. The other side may try and exploit the fact that, while you claim to be fighting for what Mom wanted, you couldn't even find the time to make it to her funeral.

c)   Use Your Financial Leverage

Estate litigation always involves expense. Sometimes you can use that to your advantage. Depending on the circumstances, your opponents may be willing to settle with you now in order to preserve their entitlement.

To illustrate this strategy, imagine that Dad is a widower. He has three sons, each of whom would be entitled to one third of his estate under his first Will. However, late in his life, Dad prepares a new Will, which cuts his eldest son out of his estate. Dad subsequently dies, and the new Will is read.

When the eldest son cannot persuade his two siblings to settle with him, he goes to see a lawyer. He wants to find out whether he has a good case to set aside Dad's new Will through a court action. The lawyer gives him the bad news: his claim is a weak one. If the eldest son proceeds with the litigation, he will be taking a serious risk.

However, from a tactical point of view, there are strategies that might help him. He may be able to use legal proceedings to leverage some settlement money from his other two siblings.

Suppose that the eldest son commences a claim seeking that the Will be set aside. As part of that claim he also demands that his brothers be removed as the executors of Dad's estate. He wants a neutral executor to be appointed to look after the estate until a court decides whether the Will is valid.

In the first court appearance, the lawyer for the eldest son is successful in obtaining a court order, which replaces the two younger brothers with a court-appointed neutral executor. That neutral executor is entitled to be paid compensation from the estate. That compensation is going to reduce the value of the estate, which the two younger brothers were expecting to divide between themselves. Those fees are an ongoing expense, which will continue to erode the estate until the matter is either settled or decided by a court.

In addition, the eldest son claims that his legal fees should be paid out of the estate, whether he wins or loses. In the end, the court will have the final say on whether these legal fees will be paid from the estate, even if the eldest son loses the Will challenge and the Will is found to be valid.

Let's assume the eldest son loses the Will challenge, but the court orders that his legal fees be paid out of the estate. Because the new Will was held to be valid, the two younger brothers are the sole beneficiaries of Dad's estate. However, the estate is reduced by the amount of the legal fees paid to their brother. In effect, the two younger brothers are paying their eldest brother's legal fees out of their own pockets. The longer the battle continues, the higher the eldest brother's legal fees and the greater the potential risk to the two younger brothers. The problem for the two brothers is that they will not know until the end of the proceedings whether the estate will be responsible for their eldest brother's legal fees.

The two younger brothers are the ones who bear the risk of being responsible for the ongoing expenses of the neutral executor and their brother's legal fees. The eldest brother has little to lose by raising these points, since he starts from the position of zero entitlement. If he loses, the cost of the litigation to the estate is irrelevant to him. He is not going to get any part of the estate anyway. However, this is a very important issue to the younger brothers because the estate that they would otherwise receive has been reduced by the costs of the litigation.

Therefore, the brothers may want to stop the ongoing expense of the neutral executor and eliminate the risk that the court may award their brother's legal fees even if he loses. There may a financial incentive to offer their brother some money now to end the litigation quickly. If the brother takes their offer and goes away, they can remove the neutral executor and take back their original position as executors. This will stop the ongoing depletion of the estate. Furthermore, the brothers will be able to breathe a sigh of relief knowing that there is no risk that they will be hit with their brother's legal bill.

Aside from the monetary considerations, there is yet one further tactical advantage in the hands of the eldest brother: time.

To the two younger siblings, the attack brought by their eldest brother transforms a routine estate administration into an expensive and drawn-out lawsuit. The siblings, who expected quick access to "their" money, will find that the estate is tied up in court. On the other hand, the eldest son, being the challenger, does not suffer from the delay; he was never going to get any money from Dad's new Will, in any event. Resolving the dispute quickly is to the benefit of the two brothers because they will be able to get their inheritance now rather than after a court battle that may take many years.

Against this background, the eldest brother may have leverage to convince his two brothers to settle.

One word of caution to potential Will challengers: a challenger may believe that he has nothing to lose by launching a lawsuit. However, if a court finds that your lawsuit is frivolous, without merit or should have been abandoned or settled, there could be very serious consequences for you. The court could order that you personally pay any expenses resulting from your lawsuit. For example, in addition to your own legal fees, you could be responsible for the fees paid to the neutral executor, as well as your opponent's legal fees and related expenses.

Therefore, it is almost always better for the parties to settle before trial because both sides have significant risks.

d)   Raise the Stakes

Here is another strategy designed to improve your bargaining position.

Using the same fact situation, now imagine that a few years before Dad died, and before making his last Will, he gave a house to each of the two younger brothers as a gift. Dad died, leaving $200,000 in the bank. The eldest child launches his attack on the Will. The brothers assume that the fight will be limited to that $200,000 in the bank. In their minds, Dad's estate does not include the two houses that he gave to them. They and their spouses believe that their homes are safe and out of bounds in any dispute over Dad's estate. All that is in dispute is the money. To them, Dad's estate is "found money" — anything they get from it is a windfall. They are willing to risk it all, knowing that they have their houses. They could live with the estate being wasted on the lawyers rather than their brother getting any part of it.

If that is how the siblings truly feel, the challenger is not in a very good bargaining position. However, the eldest brother may have some power here. Both sides examine their best case and worst case scenarios. For the two brothers, they see their best case scenario as getting Dad's $200,000. Before they hear from the eldest brother, they assume that their worst case scenario is splitting the $200,000 with the eldest brother. This does not seem to be much of a risk to them. They are prepared to fight it out and take their chances.

At the same time, the eldest brother is consulting with his lawyer. His lawyer points out that he may have an argument to set aside Dad's gifts of the homes to the two brothers. Six months before Dad gifted those homes, he had suffered a minor stroke. Perhaps this affected Dad's mental capacity to make the gifts, or because of his weakened state he was more susceptible to duress or undue influence from the brothers. If this could be proven, the brothers' homes would be returned to Dad's estate. If he was successful in challenging the Will, he would end up getting a third of the $200,000 and 1/3 of each of the brothers' houses. However, the lawyer advises him that he has a relatively weak case.

Even so, his lawyer tells him that there is still a tactical advantage for him to claim that Dad's gifts to the two brothers were invalid. His lawyer writes to the two brothers. He advises them that the eldest brother is claiming that their homes form part of Dad's estate. Since he is claiming that Dad's new Will is invalid and that the prior Will is valid, he wants 1/3 of the houses' value. This would be his entitlement under the prior Will.

Now the two brothers will have to reconsider what happens if they lose. Not only will they lose 1/3 of the $200,000, but they will also have to share the value of their homes with their eldest brother. Up to this point, they saw their homes to be "off the table" or "off limits" in the litigation. They never expected their homes to be involved in any sort of litigation. By expanding the target zone of his attack, the eldest brother raised the stakes of the lawsuit for the brothers.

This technique is not confined to houses. Another target might be a monetary gift made by the parent to his child. Similarly, a child who launches an attack on the Will should examine any joint bank accounts held between the deceased parent and one of the other children. If these transfers can be set aside, the assets will be brought back into the parent's estate; in other words, assets that the other child felt were his are up for grabs. You have upped the ante of the lawsuit.

With the stakes higher, there are risks to both sides.

The challenger exposes himself to serious legal costs if the other side doesn't back down. If the matter ends up going to court and he loses, he may pay a heavy price. As in most cases of raising the stakes, the challenger who raises them must do so with caution.

On the other hand, the defenders face ongoing uncertainty. In our example, if the brothers do not settle, they could end up losing their homes. Having this possibility hanging over their heads may be very stressful. Giving the brother a part of the estate may be a small price to pay to protect them from possibly losing their homes, and to end having to live with uncertainty for many years during the litigation.

This strategy is based on the following theory: having to give up something that you consider to be yours is much harder than giving up something that doesn't yet belong to you.

CHAPTER 8

SEE YOU IN COURT!

IF YOU CAN'T PREVENT IT, WHAT HAPPENS NEXT?

1. AN OVERVIEW OF THE ESTATE LITIGATION PROCESS

For those who have never been involved in estate litigation, one word best describes the experience: "overwhelming." This section takes you through a typical estate litigation case, explaining the steps and the process involved.

In view of the fact that the language, terms, timing and procedure may vary to some extent from jurisdiction to jurisdiction, your case may proceed in a different manner from what you are about to read.

An Example Case

Dad was living with one of his sons, Allan, who is unmarried. His other son, Barry, lives in a town an hour away, with his wife and three daughters. Dad's daughter, Cathy, lives in Australia. She left home at age 18 and has only seen Dad one time in the past 5 years and that was at Mom's funeral.

Dad's last Will gives 75% to Allan and 25% to Barry. Dad's prior Will made many years ago gave everything equally to Allan, Barry and Cathy.

When Dad died, Cathy approached her siblings about Dad's Will. Unfortunately, Cathy and her siblings could not amicably settle their differences. Cathy hired a lawyer to challenge Dad's last Will.

a)   Disclosure

The first thing that happens is that Cathy wants to get a copy of Dad's last Will, his prior Will and a list of Dad's assets. Allan, who is named as sole executor in Dad's Will, may refuse to give Cathy those documents, claiming that she is not a beneficiary and that she has no right to any information about Dad's estate. However if he doesn't give her what she is asking for, Cathy will have no choice but to sue to get the information. On the other hand, why should Allan help Cathy?

If those basic documents are not provided, Cathy will proceed with a court application to get them. As long as Cathy can show that she may be a beneficiary under Dad's *prior* Will, the court will likely order that Allan provide copies to her. Cathy must be able to show that if the last Will is not valid, she will be entitled to a part of the estate either under a prior Will or as an heir if Dad died without a Will.

b)   Objections to Dad's Will

When Cathy meets with her lawyer, he advises her about the potential grounds for challenging Dad's Will.

Cathy's first step will be to have her lawyer file a court document to advise the court that she challenges Dad's last Will. Depending on where you live, this may be called a "Notice of Objection" or a "Caveat." She will be required to outline the grounds on which she is challenging the Will. These grounds could be that Dad didn't know what he was doing when he made his last Will or that Allan pressured Dad to give him 75% of the estate. She will also have to show that she would be a beneficiary of Dad's estate if his last Will were to be found invalid. If properly filed, these documents will generally stop Allan, as executor, from getting probate and administering the estate. It should be pointed out that in a different jurisdiction, this particular step might take the form of commencing a formal lawsuit.

c)   Court Directions

Once Cathy has challenged the Will, the parties will go to a judge, who will give directions to the litigating parties.

The judge may order that Cathy has to give more detail about her claim. The judge may also order that Dad's medical records be disclosed to the parties. The judge could order that the lawyer who drafted Dad's last Will provide his notes and records to the parties and that the lawyer be asked questions under oath about Dad's mental capacity to make the last Will.

The judge will also appoint someone to administer the estate while the litigation is going on. This person is usually a neutral party whose job it is to make sure that the estate assets are protected and invested until the litigation is over. That administrator is also required to make sure that the estate pays all of Dad's outstanding taxes and debts. Sometimes, the judge may decide to appoint a bank to be the administrator during the litigation. It is common for the administrator to be compensated from the estate.

By this time, Barry may have retained his own lawyer.

What side is Barry on? Does he support Allan and uphold the last Will, where he gets 25%? Does he side with Cathy and challenge Dad's last Will in the hope that he will get 1/3 of the estate under the prior Will? Does he stay neutral and just wait on the sidelines until the fighting is over? These are decisions that Barry will have to make by the time the judge gives directions regarding the lawsuit.

In our example case, Barry decides to wait on the sidelines and not take an active part in the litigation.

d)   Discovery and Depositions

Once the judge has given directions, lawyers for each side will have an opportunity to question Cathy and Allan about Dad and his last Will.

Allan's lawyer will question Cathy about her estrangement from her dad. Cathy's lawyer will question Allan about his influence over his dad. Both lawyers will question the lawyer who drafted Dad's Will about his observations of Dad, Dad's mental capacity and any suggestions that Allan influenced his dad to make his last Will.

The lawyers may also want to question Dad's family doctor about Dad's health and dependence on Allan.

e)   Witness and Fact Gathering

The lawyers for both Cathy and Allan will be looking for witnesses who observed Dad at the time that the last Will was prepared. These may be Dad's acquaintances, friends, relatives, nurses or other caregivers.

Often, simple information is most important. How did Dad act at the family Christmas party? What hobbies did Dad have? Did Allan seem overbearing or just helpful? Did Dad ever discuss current events? Did Dad seem to be vulnerable, or dependent on Allan, because of his age or health? Did Allan keep Dad isolated and away from other people? Were there any suspicious circumstances surrounding the making of Dad's last Will? For example, was Dad in the hospital, or was Allan in the room when Dad signed his last Will?

Answers to questions about Dad's everyday life can be very influential in a Will challenge.

f)   Reviewing Medical Records and Lawyer's Notes

Medical records may be the most important evidence of all. Let's assume that Dad was in the hospital around the time of the last Will. Both sides will be reviewing the notes of the nurses and doctors to find evidence that Dad was either mentally capable or not. The lawyers will look carefully at what condition Dad was in. Was he taking medication that would impact his mental functioning, such as morphine? Was he eating properly? Was he sleeping half the day? It is quite common to see notes from the nurses and other staff referring to Dad's functioning. Sometimes, there are discussions in the notes about how alert Dad was or whether he seemed disoriented. All of these may help a judge to decide whether Dad was mentally capable of making his last Will.

The lawyer's notes should also be helpful. When the lawyer met with Dad to make the last Will, he should have kept notes of his observations. How did Dad appear? Was he able to answer questions? Did he appear to know the value of his assets? Could he explain why he was cutting Cathy out of the Will and why he was giving 75% to Allan? Was Allan present in the room when the lawyer met with Dad? Were there any indications of undue influence? Was he originally Allan's lawyer or had he been Dad's lawyer for many years?

g)   Mediation

Most cases settle before trial. The closest most cases get to anything like a "day in court," with both parties present and with a neutral party involved, is a mediation. In the jurisdiction in which Cathy and Allan are battling each other, mediation is not a mandatory step. However, there are jurisdictions where mediation is compulsory. In the example case, mediation will not occur unless both Allan and Cathy agree to be involved. As we have discussed, mediations are often very effective in resolving inheritance disputes.

A mediation is a meeting that all the lawyers, as well as Allan and Cathy (and Barry, if he decides to become involved), will attend. In addition, a neutral person called a "mediator" is present. It is common to use mediators who have experience with estates in these kinds of disputes. Former judges or experienced estate lawyers can be excellent mediators, who carry additional credibility for the parties.

The mediation typically starts with Allan, Cathy, their lawyers and the mediator in a room around a big table. If Barry is a party, he will be there too. Before the mediation, the lawyers will have filed mediation documents outlining the outstanding issues and the positions and evidence of their clients.

The mediation usually starts with an explanation of the mediation process. The mediator will explain the purpose of the mediation.

The mediator may ask Allan and Cathy to sign a mediation agreement that confirms that anything discussed in the mediation is confidential and cannot be used in a court. This permits both Allan and Cathy to be open and free and allows them and their lawyers to discuss settlement, without the risk that the opposing party will use it against them in court.

Once the mediator has introduced the process, each of the parties will usually make an opening statement. Sometimes the lawyer will aggressively state his client's position. Perhaps Allan's lawyer will point out that Cathy has been estranged from Dad for years and that she has done nothing to help her dad and therefore doesn't "deserve" anything. That is how Allan feels and what he wants expressed by his lawyer. However, by being that confrontational, Allan's lawyer may defeat the purpose of the mediation. Will Cathy want to settle when her brother has just said that she abandoned her father? Will that not just force Cathy to tell Allan that he only looked after Dad to get his money? How does either of these statements help to bring the parties together? They probably do more harm than good in terms of trying to settle the case.

However, maybe both Allan and Cathy need to express these feelings. It is often recommended, therefore, that these types of inflammatory comments be expressed in private to the mediator. Privacy creates the benefit of allowing a party to express deeply held feelings to a neutral party who can acknowledge and validate them. In addition, a skilled mediator will use these comments in a productive way to encourage settlement.

After the opening statements, each party may go into his or her own private room with his or her own lawyer. This is called a "caucus." The mediator will then go from one room to the other, trying to flesh out the parties' positions, determine the emotional underpinnings of each side, and identify where there is room to negotiate. The mediator will explore the positions of the parties to see what compromises can be made. The mediator may ask whether Allan wants to make an offer to give Cathy some part of the estate. In this case, Allan's lawyer recommends that Allan make an offer of 10% of Dad's estate to Cathy.

The mediator will then go to Cathy with Allan's offer. Cathy may make a counteroffer and so on. Back and forth the mediator will go until the parties reach a point where neither side will compromise further, or they have agreed on a settlement.

Allan and Cathy should give their best efforts to try and settle the case at mediation. For one thing, mediation is emotionally draining: Allan and Cathy will have spent the whole day dealing with their own feelings about their Dad and about each other. Each of them will have confronted the other. The day of the mediation is a very difficult day. To leave that day without the case being over, knowing that there is much more of this same type of fighting yet to come, could be a very depressing thought.

Furthermore, mediations constitute the best chance that the parties have to end the litigation. The parties are all present at a mediation and their lawyers are focused on the case. You have to remember that while your estate fight may be your only case, your own lawyer will likely have many other cases. During your mediation, your lawyer is only thinking about your case and working hard to resolve it. If you fail to resolve it then, your lawyer will be moving on to other cases until at least the next step in your litigation.

If Allan and Cathy are able to agree on a compromise, the lawyers will likely document the agreement right then and there. The agreement may specify who has to do what to effect the settlement, when the payments have to be made and who is going to be responsible for finalizing the administration of the estate. If Barry was not present at the mediation, his consent may still be necessary if the agreement affects his rights in the estate.

In some cases, the court will have to approve the settlement, such as where there are minor or incapable beneficiaries. In those cases, the agreement is conditional on obtaining the approval of the court.

There can be a great deal of pressure in documenting the settlement. Usually, the agreement is not completed until after a long day of mediation. The signed agreement is binding on all of the parties and usually cannot be changed. Therefore, the parties must be careful to include all necessary provisions in the agreement.

We have often seen mediations where all of the financial details have been worked out and the agreement is ready to sign, but at the last moment one of the parties raises a side issue. In this case, it happens to be Dad's coin collection. Cathy raises this issue and insists on receiving the coin collection as part of the settlement. Allan is upset that they have had all day to deal with this issue and that his sister is raising it just before the agreement is to be signed. A settlement which was so close could fall apart over this one little issue. To avoid these last-minute issues, both parties should properly prepare for the mediation. Cathy and Allan should plan out what they hope to achieve in a settlement. Late surprises are never good.

h)   Pre-Trial Conference

Assuming that the case is not resolved at mediation, the next step is a pre-trial, which is a meeting between the lawyers and a judge. Sometimes the clients are present at the pre-trial as well. The judge will give his views on the likelihood of success for both sides.

The judge may tell Cathy that she is going to have a hard time proving a lack of capacity based on Dad's medical records and the evidence of the lawyer who drafted Dad's last Will. However he may point out that Allan seems to have been influencing his dad and that Allan might lose the undue influence case.

The pre-trial judge may be looking for ways of settling the case involving just the lawyers. Other times, the judge will want to speak directly with the clients. For example, the judge may call Cathy in and tell her directly what he thinks about her case. This might be a reality check for Cathy, who up to this point believed that there was no way she could lose. Her "wake-up" call comes to her when she hears a judge tell her that she has a poor case. The opinion of a judge at a pre-trial can be a real "wake-up" call for clients.

If the case is not settled at the pre-trial, the judge will ask the lawyers for a list of witnesses and the expected time that they anticipate the trial will take. The judge may also deal with administrative motions, such as requests for disclosure or the order in which the court will hear the argument of both sides. In the jurisdiction in which Allan is fighting Cathy, the judge who hears the pre-trial is forbidden to hear the case when it comes to trial. Another judge must be the one to hear the case at trial.

i)   Settlement Offers

While the parties have prepared for and attended a pre-trial, there may still be last-minute attempts at resolving the dispute. Each side may want to make settlement offers to the other for a number of reasons:

1.   The trial involves the most intensive amount of lawyer's time. This translates into being the most expensive step in the litigation. If Cathy and Allan can settle the case before trial, a significant amount of legal fees will be saved.

2.   Trials are great risks; no case is a sure thing. In fact, we often tell our clients that even with the very best case, you have only a 50-50 chance. Every judge is different and every judge has his or her own point of view. Most estate cases are fought where the stakes are all or nothing. When you go to trial, both sides have a chance to end up with nothing. If you can eliminate the risk by settling your claim for something before a judge gives you nothing, you are better off.

3.   Settlements are not admissions of being wrong, or worse, of the other side being right. They should never be viewed as indications of who is right or who is wrong. You will always know, deep in your heart, that you are right. A settlement does not change that. All it means is that you have gone far enough, taken the necessary steps, completed all possible investigations and made the best efforts to satisfy yourself that you have done the right thing for what you are fighting for, whether it is yourself, your family or your deceased parent's memory.

4.   Your day in court is not what you think. You may believe that once a judge hears your side, the judge will automatically side with you. Technicalities, rules of evidence, legal arguments and precedents all limit the ability of judges to hear the "whole" case. The lawyers for the other side will slant the evidence to support the case of their client. Watching a trial as a party to litigation can be a very frustrating experience. Evidence which you believe is inaccurate is often brought out and seemingly believed by the judge. Judges always expect that there are two sides to every story.

5.   Judges don't find "truth," they only find the facts based on what comes from evidence which is admitted in court. In most cases, no one knows what really happened. Each side has his or her own strongly held beliefs. The only person who really knows what the Will meant, or what was really intended, is no longer with us. The Will-maker has obviously passed away, and cannot testify.

6.   The court is an open forum and the record of a trial is a public record. Anyone can, after the trial, read about your personal issues, the family's secrets and "dirty laundry," which may have been kept privately within the family before the matter came to trial. Now they are all exposed for business associates, competitors and family and friends to read about.

7.   Being cross-examined in front of a judge in a courtroom is not a pleasant experience. Be fully aware that if you are a party to this kind of a case, in all likelihood you will be thoroughly cross-examined by the opposing lawyer. Cross examinations can, in some cases, be very lengthy. Some witnesses or parties can find themselves in the witness box, in front of the judge and everyone in court, for hours and in some cases even days.

8.   Some people also don't make good witnesses. They may be defensive, evasive or not comfortable in a courtroom. Judges have to determine, based only on what they see and hear in the courtroom, whether a witness's explanations or observations are accurate or not. This is done by observing the demeanour of the witness and his body language, along with what the witness actually says. The witness may be telling an accurate story, but if the judge does not believe it, the witness will not help the case of the party who brought that witness to court.

9.   At trial you must pull out all the stops to win your case. You may have to involve friends and family as witnesses, who often do not want to come to court and take sides. In

most cases, they just want to stay out of it. However, if they have important evidence that will help your case, they will have to be called to court. It can be very uncomfortable to have to subpoena a friend or relative under threats that they will be in contempt of court if they don't show up.

10. In the jurisdiction in which Allan and Cathy are fighting, making a settlement offer may influence the amount of legal fees that the court will award after the trial. For example, as a proposal, Cathy offers that Allan gets 50% of the estate instead of 75%, as set out in Dad's last Will. If Allan loses at trial and, therefore, only receives 1/3 of the estate under the prior Will, the court may force Allan to pay more of Cathy's legal fees. The logic behind this legal rule is based on the fact that Allan rejected Cathy's offer and chose instead to go to trial. At trial, he was awarded less than what Cathy offered him in the first place. The legal rule is also based on the reality that court time is very precious. Any party who burdens the court with a case that could have been settled, will be penalized with costs.

11. One of the benefits of early settlement may be that it averts further damage to the relationship between the siblings and the rest of the family. A settlement later in the proceedings may work financially. However, often this financial resolution may come too late to salvage what is left of the relationship between the siblings. The hostility that has been unleashed between the siblings during the lengthy litigation may have already done irreparable damage.

j) Trial

At the beginning of the trial, both sides will have the opportunity to make opening statements. These statements summarize for the judge the theory of each side's case.

The lawyers will have arranged to have their witnesses available to give evidence. These witnesses include the parties themselves, as well as other non-expert witnesses.

Depending on the type of case, experts such as doctors, lawyers or handwriting specialists will be called as witnesses.

For example, Cathy decides to call an expert to testify on Dad's mental capacity. Her lawyer hires a forensic psychiatrist. He never met Dad, but he specializes in the area of mental capacity. This expert reviews Dad's medical records and provides an opinion to the court. In the expert's view, based on Dad's medical condition, Dad did not have the mental capacity to make his last Will. Allan decides to call his own capacity expert, who disagrees with Cathy's expert. In the end, the judge will have to decide whether either of the experts is helpful in deciding the case.

These professionals will normally charge the party calling them for attending court on his or her behalf. Experts are usually very expensive to have as witnesses. They normally are required to file a written report as well as to testify live in court.

In estate cases, there are usually a substantial number of documents that will be put into evidence. As they are put into evidence, the judge assigns an exhibit number to each of them.

The lawyers will also put together their own "briefs," which contain copies of relevant prior cases or precedents that will help the judge come to a decision.

Once both sides have produced all of their evidence, each side will have the opportunity to make final submissions. These involve summarizing the evidence and the applicable law.

The judge will usually "reserve" his or her decision. This means that the judge will take some time to write a judgment explaining who wins and who loses. In addition, the judge may make a decision about who should pay the legal fees of the lawyers involved. It can take many months for the judge to finalize his or her decision before it is released to the parties.

k)   Appeal

If either party believes that the trial judge made a mistake in his or her decision, that party usually has the right to appeal the judgment.

An appeal is not the same as a new trial. There is no evidence given in an appeal. The appeal judges use the same evidence that was used in the trial. The appeal judges will determine whether the trial judge made a mistake in applying the law to the facts.

Sometimes offers of settlement will be made by the parties to resolve the matter without having to go through with the appeal. For the side that won at trial, settlement eliminates the risk that the appeal court could overturn the decision. For the losing side, they get something from a settlement at this stage. They also avoid the risk of spending "good money after bad" on the appeal.

CHAPTER 9

"WINNING" ESTATE LITIGATION

Rarely can the winner of a Family War declare that his or her victory was absolute. You must look long and hard to find someone who takes a brother or sister all the way through the court system, completely conquers them, and simply doesn't care about the emotional fallout that such a victory leaves in its wake. There is almost never an absolute winner. The fact that family members are fighting means that the War will have a cost. Are you a winner if the victory means destroyed relationships with other family members or feelings of shame or guilt if you feel that you have let your parents down? These costs will continue long after the litigation ends and the lawyers are paid.

One situation that drove this last point home occurred when a distraught woman tried in her own way to deal with her pain as she told us her tragic story on a call-in radio show. In a nutshell, this is what she had to say:

Her Dad was a farmer who lost his wife when still a relatively young man. Then he ran into financial difficulties and had to raise her and her baby brother all on his own. She turned 19 as her Dad was still struggling to make ends meet. To protect the family, he had his lawyer put the farm in her name. In this way, if he ran into further trouble at least no creditors could ever take the farm.

As the years passed, her brother began working on the farm, and it prospered. When Dad died, his Will left the farm to her brother.

What happened next? They both found out that because the farm was registered in her name, she was the legal owner. If that was the case, her brother had no claim to the farm under Dad's Will. She wanted her brother to buy the farm from her or at least pay her a fair share. He refused. He said it was Dad's intention to give the farm to him. After that, the lawyers became involved. There was a heated battle between them and they could not resolve anything. She ultimately won the case and took the farm. She sold it to a developer.

She was close to tears when she was describing this on the radio. She told us that at the time she won she felt vindicated and empowered. She believed that she deserved the victory; the fact that her brother was not speaking to her seemed to be a fair price to pay at the time. Besides, she was sure that with the passage of time, matters would resolve themselves.

Her expectation of a reconciliation faded after months of silence between her and her brother. Then one night, her brother's wife was on the phone, asking her if she would come to her brother's funeral. Her brother had been killed in a car accident—her baby brother, her only brother.

What had she been thinking? She told us that she would burn every dollar she got from that farm if she could only turn back the hands of the clock. She was devastated. She tried so very many ways to purge the pain and guilt. She was crying as she told us that all of this would stay with her for the rest of her life.

This account demonstrates one example of a person winning financially and legally, but suffering a loss because she could not live with the result.

Your lawyer may be able to assess your case from a legal point of view, but to come closer to a true victory, you must be able to assess whether you can live with the result you are trying to achieve. In order to assess this, you might turn your mind to the fact that eventually, whether through court or settlement, the litigation will end, and your life will carry on beyond that. Before an estate dispute gets out of control, ask yourself these questions:

- Will a victory in court cause me to lose sleep at night?

- How will I feel if my victory causes my brother to have health problems, or to lose his wife, or his home, or causes him to declare bankruptcy?

- Will the fact that my court case becomes public cause me grief, notoriety or embarrassment?

- Will I be labelling myself as the person who betrayed my family? Will I be unleashing family secrets, confidential business information and "dirty laundry" to hostile eyes and ears?

- How will I explain it to my children, to my nieces and nephews, and to other relatives, who were not personally involved in the dispute?

- How will my own children be affected if I widen a rift within my family instead of healing it?

- How will I cope with feelings that I may have disappointed my parents in fighting with my siblings?

- Did my parents really want part of their hard-earned estate to go to lawyers?

Even if your lawyer tells you that you have an excellent legal case, you may still have misgivings because you may not be able to live with the result of a Family War. Instead of all-out legal victory, perhaps a settlement that everyone can live with is really winning the Family War.

Sometimes there are pressures from other people in your life, such as your spouse or child, to go the distance and fight for everything you can get.

"You deserve more!" "Don't give your brother a penny!" These calls to war may be well-intentioned and seemingly supportive, but in the end you are the one who will have to live with the fallout of your decision. The sibling involved in the fight is your sibling, not theirs.

Remember the good days together — the family vacations, the walks to school, and how you helped each other get through tough times.

Ultimately, you are the one who may lose the Family War.

CHAPTER 10

SOME DANGEROUS ASSUMPTIONS

1.   Estate litigation proceeds quickly, like on TV.

In reality, the process of litigation is lengthy, often consuming months, and even years, until it is completed. Every step is drawn out. When your lawyer writes to the lawyer for the other side, it may take weeks for the other lawyer to write back to him or her. If you need documents from hospitals or banks, it could take months until the documents are received. Court dates are rarely immediate and often adjourned. You can assume that, in most jurisdictions, it will take at least two years for the case to get to trial.

2.   All my legal fees will be paid from the estate.

Historically, in many jurisdictions, the legal fees of all of the parties were regularly paid from the estate, regardless of whether that party won or lost the case. However, nowadays courts are much more reluctant to have the estate pay the costs where one side is clearly wrong. If the court doesn't award costs out of the estate, your legal fees will come out of your inheritance or out of your own pocket.

3.   The real truth will come out at trial.

Your story may be the truth, but the judge will be hearing at least one other side of the story from your opponent. The judge may choose to believe your opposing party. Because of legal rules of evidence, a judge may not always hear everything you want him to hear. Based on the facts that he or she is allowed to consider and the way the evidence is presented, the judge may make a decision which may be very different from the "truth" as you see it. Some lawyers say that even if you think you have the best case in the world, you still have a 50% chance of losing.

4.   Charities will not challenge Wills or sue executors.

People assume that charities, when named as beneficiaries, will not become involved in litigation and will be happy to receive anything at all. Many charities are like that. However, there are other charities who do challenge Wills. They may allege that when your mom made a new Will reducing what the charity gets, she was being unduly influenced or was not mentally capable. They may also sue you as the executor if you invest poorly. They may also challenge the amount of compensation you claim as an executor.

5.   My life will go on as normal during an estate dispute.

Clients often underestimate how much personal time is required during an estate dispute. Even though your lawyer will present the case to the court, you will have to invest a significant amount of time in providing information about the case to your lawyer. You may have to do the legwork to uncover some of the information that the lawyer needs.

Although some of the work can be done through faxes, emails and telephone conversations, you will have to be physically present at certain times in the process. This may mean taking days off work and reshuffling personal schedules.

At various stages of the litigation you will have to come face to face with family members who are opposing you. You will be telling and retelling stories that re-open wounds each time they are recounted. Even though you are not meeting with lawyers every day, the litigation is on your mind every day. It is often all consuming. Many people find that they can't even start their grieving until the litigation has ended.

6.   If I do my best as executor, I will not be sued.

Your honesty and best efforts are no guarantee that you will be immune from attack from the beneficiaries. Doing your best may not be good enough if you don't do it right.

7.   My own brother would never sue me.

One of the first reactions for many clients is one of surprise: "I can't believe this is happening!" Typical pressures that can push your loving brother to attack you may include:

* Pressure from his spouse;

* Personal financial pressures, which influence him to seek funds from any source, even if it means fighting his own brother for a greater share of his parent's estate;

* Unresolved emotional issues: you may have forgotten, or may be totally unaware, that your brother has unresolved feelings of hurt or bitterness towards the family. The Family War becomes an outlet for the pain that has been festering inside him for years.

8.   Because Mom has a Will, there won't be an estate battle.

Her Will might smooth out the process of administering the estate. However we have seen how problems and ill feelings can develop from what Mom overlooked, misinterpreted, ignored or failed to consider.

9.   Because Dad is not wealthy, no one will fight.

Fights often occur over items of sentimental value found in Dad's home. Estate disputes are often over memories, not just money.

10. Because Mom left the same amount to each of us, everyone will get along.

Being treated the same in Mom's Will does not always mean that each child will see it as being *fair*. The child who spent more time caring for Mom or the one who didn't get money for college may feel that getting the same amount as his or her siblings in Mom's Will is unfair. This child may have a legal ground to challenge the equal distribution.

CHAPTER 11

20 FREQUENTLY ASKED QUESTIONS

1. Dad died and I am positive that my brother had borrowed money from him and never paid it back. How do I prove it? Is it deducted from his share?

Proving that this debt is still outstanding may be difficult, especially if the matter has to go to court. Without hard proof, it will be your word against his. Hopefully, Dad kept a record of the money he lent, supported by a promissory note or other evidence of debt. If there is evidence of the debt, the court might look to your brother to prove that he paid the money back to your Dad.

Generally, debts owing by a beneficiary to the deceased have to be repaid or else they can be deducted from the share of the estate going to that beneficiary.

2. I am a co-executor of Dad's estate with my uncle. We cannot agree on what to do with the estate, and in the meantime, the estate assets are declining in value. What do I do?

Executors must act together unless the Will says otherwise. If there truly is a deadlock, you may each need your own lawyer. If the matter is incapable of being resolved and court proceedings are initiated by one or the other of you, the court may have to decide the matter. The court may order that one or both of you be removed and might even order that you or your uncle be replaced by a neutral person or financial institution.

3.   My mom appointed me and my brother as "joint and several" powers of attorney. I don't trust my brother. How do I make sure that he can't do something with Mom's money behind my back?

Being appointed "severally" means that each of the "attorneys" appointed in the Power of Attorney can act on his or her own without the consent of the other. It would be a good idea to notify the banks and request that they advise you of any transactions made by your brother. As an "attorney" you are entitled to have information about the accounts. Writing to your brother suggesting mutual co-operation is also a good idea. With this documentation, you will be able to show the court that you were trying to be reasonable.

4.   I was living in my dad's house when he died. Dad wanted me to be able to continue living in the house, but now his executors are trying to sell it. Can I stop them?

Executors are generally entitled to sell any assets that were not specifically given away in the Will. If you were not named as the beneficiary of the house in the Will, the executors probably have the right to sell it. You may want to consider making an offer to purchase the house using your share of the estate.

If you were living rent free in the house, you may be your Dad's dependant and may be entitled to ask a court to let you stay in the house.

5.   My dad died 9 months ago and I still have not received my share of his estate. How long should it take until I get my money?

Depending upon the complexity of the estate involved, it could take about a year or so to administer the estate and to make a first distribution to the beneficiaries.

6. Aside from receiving a copy of my sister's Will, I have not heard what's happening with the estate. When is it appropriate for me to contact the executor to find out the status of the estate?

You have the right to contact the executor at any time. As a beneficiary, you are entitled to know about the status of the administration of the estate and your sister's assets. However you must be realistic in your expectations. As a rule of thumb, you would be acting reasonably if you asked for a status report every three months or so, unless there is a situation that clearly makes this estate a special case.

7. My sister, my brother and I are the three beneficiaries of my mom's estate. I don't need the money and I want my share to go to my sister, but not my brother. How can I do this?

One option is to "disclaim" or "surrender" your share in her estate. However, that will result in your share being divided equally between your sister and your brother. Another option would be to take your share and then give it to your sister. Before taking these steps you should obtain professional tax and legal advice.

8. My dad left a note to me that he wants me to get his house. Is that valid?

Depending on where you live, if the note was entirely in your Dad's handwriting and signed by him, it may be valid as a "holograph Will." If it was not signed, it is not a valid Will.

9. Dad owed a lot of money when he died. As the executor, am I responsible to pay his debts out of my own pocket if there is not enough in the estate to pay them?

An executor is generally responsible to use only the assets of the estate to satisfy the deceased's debts. If there is not enough money to pay all of the debts in full, you will want to contact a lawyer to advise you on who and how much to pay to the deceased's creditors.

10. Mom left burial instructions in her Will that said that she wanted to be cremated. My brother is the executor and he refuses to cremate her. Can he do that?

In most jurisdictions, funeral or burial directions in a Will are not binding on an executor. As a result, if your mom lived in one of these jurisdictions, your brother will have the final say on how to deal with Mom's burial.

11. I know that Dad made a recent Will, but I cannot find it anywhere. What do I do?

If you suspect that Dad made a Will with a lawyer, you can put an advertisement in the local lawyer's magazine asking if any lawyer in that area made a Will for your father.

12. I am 65 and my new husband is 83. His kids think that I am a gold digger. How do I protect myself from his children when he dies?

You better be ready for a fight. Children who are upset at their parent's subsequent marriage, and whose inheritance may be substantially diminished because of that marriage, will often attack the new spouse on as many fronts as they can. They might even attack the validity of the marriage itself.

You should be arming yourself with as much evidence as you can find to confirm that your husband knew what he was doing, including getting a mental capacity assessment if possible. Documenting your life together is also a good idea. Pictures, cards and other tangible evidence of your relationship will help you.

13. Dad's Will left me the right to live in his house for the rest of my life. What are my rights, and can my estate be sued for anything when I die?

You have the right, during your life, to stay in that house free from interference from the executors. For example, an executor is not entitled to enter the house without proper notice to you. Dad's Will would normally set out who is responsible for the house expenses, such as utilities, insurance and maintenance. If the Will makes the expenses your responsibility, you must pay them. You must also keep the house in good condition and not damage it beyond reasonable wear and tear. You should check that the proper insurance is in place for both the house and your personal effects.

If, when you die, the house is significantly damaged, meaning more than usual wear and tear, your estate may be responsible to Dad's estate for repairing that damage.

14. My dad just died and his Will divided his estate between me and my sister. However my sister passed away a year ago, leaving her husband and two children. Do I get Dad's whole estate or does my sister's share go to her family?

This depends on the wording of Dad's Will. Some Wills contain a "gift over" clause. This provision might say, for example, that if your sister died before your Dad, her share goes to someone else, like her children or her husband. If there is no "gift over" clause, and depending on the wording of your Dad's Will and where he lived, her share could either go to you, or be divided among her surviving family.

15. My mom's rings are gone from her home. In the Will, she left these rings to me. Do I get the equivalent value in money?

Depending on where you live, if these rings were sold, lost, destroyed or given away before your mom died, the gift of the rings in the Will is void. Therefore, you are *not* entitled to the equivalent value in money unless the Will specifically says so.

216

16.   My dad died recently. He was living with another woman in her condo. She is claiming that she owns all of the furniture in the condo. How do I prove that my dad owned some of the furniture?

Knowing something and proving it are two very different things. While you may know that your Dad purchased the furniture, unless you have receipts it may be difficult to prove. Check old credit card statements, if you can find them. Even if you can prove that your Dad bought them, the woman might claim that your Dad gave them to her as a "gift" before he died.

17.   I live with my mom. When my mom dies, I am afraid my brother will try and get into the house. Can I stop him?

If the house is in your Mom's name when she dies, her executor is entitled to take possession of her assets, including her home. If your brother is your Mom's executor, he will have the right to come into the house. If he is not the executor, he may not have the right to go into the house.

18.   My dad died yesterday and I was named under his Power of Attorney. Can I get access to his bank accounts before the bank freezes them?

As soon as your Dad died, the Power of Attorney was no longer effective. Therefore, you cannot legally access his bank accounts after his death unless you were also named as an executor in his Will.

19. My uncle is the executor of my dad's estate and he wants to sell our family cottage, which was specifically left to me in Dad's Will. I want to keep it in the family. Can I stop him?

In most jurisdictions, the law provides that if the cottage was specifically left to you in the Will, your uncle cannot sell it without your consent. The only exception would be if he needs to sell it to pay the debts of the estate.

20. Mom left my brother everything in the Will, because he promised that he would "take care of me." He is spending all of the inheritance on himself. Is there anything I can do?

In some special circumstances, you could make a claim that the money was given to your brother to be held in trust for you based on his promises to your mother. These are difficult but not impossible claims.

CHAPTER 12

ESTATE TERMS IN SIMPLE LANGUAGE

Accounting – a list of what has happened to each asset of an estate, what money has come into the estate and where the estate assets have gone.

Administrator – the person appointed by the court to administer an estate where the deceased left no Will. This is also known as a "personal representative" or an "estate trustee without a Will."

Attorney – the person appointed under a Power of Attorney to manage financial affairs or make health care decisions. In this book, Attorney does not mean lawyer.

Beneficiary – a person or charity who is entitled to receive money, assets or personal property from an estate.

Capacity – the mental ability to make decisions, such as managing one's financial affairs or health care, getting married, making gifts, or signing a Will, or Power of Attorney.

Challenger – a person who challenges the validity of a gift, Will or Power of Attorney.

Caveat – the Court Document that indicates that someone is challenging the Will. This may also be known as an "Objection."

Deceased – a person who has died. Also know as the "decedent".

Estate – the assets owned by the deceased at the time of death, which are administered by the executor or administrator. This will not include assets that pass automatically on death, such as assets with named beneficiaries or assets held in joint names.

Executor – the person appointed in a Will to administer an estate. This is also known as a "personal representative" or an "estate trustee with a Will."

Fiduciary Obligation – An executor's responsibility to act only in the best interests of the beneficiaries or those with legal entitlement to estate assets.

Heir – a relative, specified under the law, who is entitled to receive a portion or all of an estate when the deceased dies without a Will.

Holograph Will – a handwritten Will. The Will must be completely in the handwriting of the deceased and signed by him or her. There is no need for witnesses. In some jurisdictions, a Holograph Will is a valid Will.

Intestacy – Dying without a Will, e.g. Dad died "intestate."

Joint ownership – assets with two or more owners that are automatically transferred to the surviving joint owner(s) when one owner dies.

Probate – The certification by a court that a Will is valid and confirmation of the authority of the executor.

Testator – the person who makes a Will. In this book, sometimes called the "Will-maker."

Testate – dying with a Will.

Trust – a Trust involves two groups of people, a trustee (in a Will he or she may be referred to as an "executor"), who manages and invests the money, and a beneficiary who may be ultimately entitled to receive the money at some point in the future. A Will is a Trust. The executor is the trustee, who distributes the money to the beneficiaries.

Trustee – a person who administers a Trust for the benefit of the beneficiaries. An executor is a trustee who is appointed in a Will.

Undue Influence – significant coercion forcing a person to name another person as a beneficiary.

Will – the document that appoints the executor and names the beneficiaries of the estate.

Are you in, or about to be in, a Family War?

Visit *The Family War* website for a referral to Estate lawyers in your jurisdiction.

www.thefamilywar.com